The Reflection of my Journey to the Republic of South Sudan

Manyang Malet Manyang

ISBN 978-0-6486541-7-9
© Malet Manyang Manyang, 2019

Published by Africa World Books Pty. Ltd.
(www.africaworldbooks.com)

All rights reserved. No part of this publication may be reproduced, stored in a retrieval system, or transmitted, in any form, or by any means, electronic, mechanical, photocopying, recording or otherwise, without the prior permission of the publishers.

This book is sold subject to the conditions that it shall not, by way of trade or otherwise, be lent, re-sold, hired out or otherwise circulated without the publisher's prior consent in any form of binding or cover other than in which it is published and without a similar condition including the condition being imposed on the subsequent purchaser.

Design and typesetting: Africa World Books

Acknowledgements

I want to say thank you to those who helped me to write this book especially to my editors Peter Dodd and Abraham Jongroor who is a South Sudanese man who went through difficulties like I did. Without you guys, this book would not be readable. Thank you for your time and enjoy the rest of your life.

I view life as a journey. A journey that may unexpectedly end up short or little bit long. Some die young, some get older and some go unborn. Life is unfinished business. Generations come and generations go, but no one ever gets everything right. Certainly, there is no satisfaction dedicated to life's journey. The end is death and everything stems from its beginnings and endings are equivocal and ambiguous. Life is always questionable: who, what, when, where and why? Life is unfinished but not be left undone.

A Note from the Publisher

The publisher wishes to acknowledge and thank Dr Douglas H. Johnson for his invaluable help and support for Africa World Books and its mission of preserving and promoting African cultural and literary traditions and history. Dr Johnson and fellow historians have been instrumental in ensuring that African people remain connected to their past and their identity. Africa World Books is proud to carry on this mission.

PART ONE

Kenya and Kakuma Refugee Camp

1990 to 2005

Chapter 1

In May 1983, the second Sudanese Civil War broke out. Approximately two and a half million people got killed and thousands more were displaced within the Sudan region.

Many children from ages eight to eighteen were forced to flee their villages. There were children who didn't make it out of Sudan —most likely enslaved or killed. I had not been born yet but I heard a lot of stories from my father, my uncles and the rest of my elders from my community: it was a heavy war.

Thousands of refugees fled east to Ethiopia for safety. Many died on the journey from dehydration, starvation, animal attacks, etc. Exactly eight years later war then broke out in Ethiopia and all the Sudanese refugees who were seeking shelter and protection were again forced out. A lot of them lost their lives on their way back to Sudan due to many things such as infectious diseases, starvation, animals' attack and drowning in rivers that they needed to cross.

After walking hundreds of miles back to the Sudan, they only had a limited amount of time there. War was still raging during this time and it wasn't safe. As the danger in Sudan continued to rise, the Lost Boys were forced to leave again. This time to go to Kenya, to what would become the Kakuma Refugee Camp in Northern Kenya.

On the journey to Kenya, many more refugees died. Some would just sit down and die where they lay from starvation, dehydration and exhaustion.

The Reflection of my Journey to the Republic of South Sudan

After walking for approximately 700 to 1000 miles, most of the refugees reached the Kakuma Refugee Camp in Kenya including my family. It was 1992. Only about half of the people survived the journey and made it to the Kakuma Refugee Camp.

In the Kakuma Refugee Camp refugees were at least given medical attention and food, clean water, and temporary shelters to live in.

Throughout this entire journey I was protected—I was an infant. I was born in 1990 in the Itang Refugee Camp in Ethiopia. I don't really know or remember much about it because I was so young. I could not contribute to anything that could possibly help my family but was dependent on them. I didn't know much about Kakuma either till I turned tens when I started to learn more about it. The war between North and South Sudan is a war many of the South Sudanese people who had witnessed it would never forget especially those who were born during and before it.

In 1992 after my family and other South Sudanese crossed borders, rivers, mountains and deserts looking for a safe place from the war, they arrived at the Kakuma Refugees Camp, the place they called temporary settlement though it wasn't that safe. The United Nations High Commissioner for Refugees (UNHCR), Red Cross and other humanitarian agencies organised free transportation for these desperate Sudanese refugees from Lokichokio a border town between Sudan and Kenya. The Kakuma Refugee Camp was bit farther away from the Sudan-Kenya border. It wasn't just a simple pick up and drop off operation as some refugees tried to walk but it was long way to go and the UN security vehicles had to pick them up on the way. I was still a very little boy, but my father and the rest of my elders told me about all this sad journey.

Chapter 2

The Kakuma Refugee Camp is located in the Turkana District of the north-western region of Kenya, 120 kilometers from the Lodwar District Headquarters and 95 kilometers from Lokichokio, on the Kenya-Sudan border.

The Kakuma Refugee Camp accommodated refugees who were forcefully dislodged from their home countries of origin by their governments. It was established in 1992 to serve Sudanese refugees, as a second settlement after they were forced out of Ethiopia in May 1991, and then expanded to accommodate more refugees from Somalia, Ethiopia, Burundi, Congo, Eritrea, Uganda and Rwanda. According to the current UNHCR statistics, the camp population now stands closer to 180,000 refugees which is almost doubling the local population.

The local Kenyan population is largely comprised of nomadic and pastoralists from the Turkana community. According to the 1999 Kenya Census, the local Kenyan population of Kakuma town was about 97,114.

The Kakuma Refugee Camp is administered by the United Nations High Commissioner for Refugees (UNHCR) in conjunction with the Kenyan Authority and supported by refugee representatives which always comes from South Sudanese background as they are the majority in the camp. The UNHCR is assisted in delivering its duties by a wide range of organizations, including the World Food Program (WFP), the International Organization for Migration (IOM), the Lutheran World Federation (LWF), the

The Reflection of my Journey to the Republic of South Sudan

International Rescue Committee (IRC), the Jesuit Refugee Services (JRS), the National Council of Churches of Kenya.

Life in the semi-arid desert environment of Kakuma was rather challenging. The area has always been full of problems, dust storms, high temperatures, poisonous spiders, snakes, and scorpions and with the humid environment come outbreaks of malaria, cholera, and other hardships. The average daytime temperature was 40 degrees Celsius, or 104 degrees Fahrenheit. I have not been back since I left the camp.

Due to their legal situation and local environmental conditions, refugees are largely unable to support themselves with income-generating activities. The semi-arid climate of Kakuma is ill-suited to agriculture, while restrictions on employment deter refugees from job-seeking. Those who work with the NGOs receive a small incentive payment for their work, but incentive staff represent only a fraction of the refugee population.

Living inside the camp is both prison and exile. Once admitted, refugees do not have freedom to move about the country but are required to obtain Movement Passes from the UNHCR and the Kenyan Government.

Chapter 3

I was a refugee in Kakuma for a good fourteen years. Kakuma as a place is not conducive for human life because of the severe weather, the windy and dusty conditions and the extreme heat throughout the year.

Insecurity is another issue facing refugees in Kakuma. I remember that there were several times I had to stay up the whole night with my relatives just to make sure that we kept watch for the bandits.

It was terrible because we didn't have any weapons to protect ourselves. All we had to do was to shout at them just to make the bandits think that people were still awake and that really worked.

The question which was in mind of every refugee was "Who is terrorizing us?" Was it the host community or the police who were supposed to protect the refugees? That was difficult to determine though we had some suspicions. Luckily some of the refugees managed to catch some of the culprits and surprisingly it turned out that some policemen and locals were involved.

That was how simple life was back in those days. I would love to go back to Kakuma one day. Some of my friends and relatives are still living there and so I feel very attached to that place. Life was really hard there, but it made me who I am today and so I am proud to be a refugee from Kakuma.

While living in Kakuma my life there wasn't easy at all as some people might imagine. It was a terrible life but a bit better than other individuals of my age who were living there without both their parents especially those who lost their parents during the war and or on the journey from Ethiopia back to Sudan and from Sudan to Kenya. My life was far better compared to theirs because my both parents were there with me and my father used to work with sport as a soccer referee and use incentives, he received to support us.

Chapter 4

In a real sense there was a little change after arrival to Kakuma. In Kakuma the UNHCR was able to provide free schools, medicines, shelters and water. From that angle, Kakuma worked well, but one thing I didn't like about Kakuma was the weather: it was too hot.

Going to school in Kakuma was hard because of the weather and food. Sitting in a classroom that is made of bricks and corrugated iron was like sitting beside an open oven. The classrooms were extremely hot and overcrowded. This situation encouraged students to stay out of class and have no breakfast or lunch. Studying with an empty stomach made most students not focus on their studies.

We started school under the trees though it was a refugee camp under management of the UNHCR. We used to sit under the tree and write on the sand as our exercise book and remember every single word for the exams. Teachers used to write words on the black board and we would then copy them by writing them in the sand. Most of us started to write and read by writing on the sand until the UNHCR and other organizations was able to provide us with all the necessary school materials such as pens, pencils, benches and exercise books.

The other challenge we faced was punishment as the teachers used to discipline us when we got to school late. They made us kneel on hot sand or made us carry two heavy rocks in our hands in the hot sun. Sometimes they even made us pick up rubbish within the school compound or clean up the school's toilets.

The discipline was very high across all the schools. Most of the teachers were not friendly with students at all and were intimidating.

As a child growing up in the refugee camp, there were a lot of things that made life feel unworthy which implies that being a refugee child is hard. You can't fulfil any of your dreams at all like most of the children whose dreams were to have a better education or better life.

The things that made life very hard started with simple things. There wasn't enough food to eat whether it was breakfast or lunch and this was an addition to hot weather which was already a huge problem for us.

Being a refugee was and is a challenge. Refugees face things like not getting enough food, water or even life-threatening situations from the elements in the surrounding environment including the host communities and this is still the case at the Kakuma Refugee Camp even as I write this. Death at the hands of members of the local/host community was like malaria amidst us. We once faced a malaria outbreak and were not getting enough medicine to get a full course of treatment.

Chapter 5

In 2003 Uncle Machar Mayen's wedding took place. During that time women were preparing food at night before the wedding day next morning. Because it was night and some of them felt sleepy, they had to entertain themselves by singing traditionnel songés which is a popular practice among women when such an occasion is about to commence. I was very young at the time, about thirteen. I was just playing around with my childhood friends including my younger brothers near this group of women.

In the middle of night, the local members of the Turkana community who normally threatened us with guns came into the compound with guns. While walking toward us one of my cousins spotted them and then she started screaming loudly "Turkana, Turkana are here in the compound! Run for cover!"

Everyone then ran away and hid at the back of the mud huts. There was a lot of screaming everywhere in the compound. The bandits tried to shoot but luckily there was no one injured as the magazine slipped out of the gun and the bullets were lost in the dark. The bandits began to panic and began to run away. I believe they didn't have any spares in their possession.

They took the food that was prepared by the women and other important belongings. Everyone was badly scared and even my body was shaking on the ground.

Early in the morning we woke up and my father walked around to assess the damage done during the ordeal and he found a bullet on the ground. He picked it up and showed it to the members of the family who were still there. That was my first time seeing a bullet in my entire life. It was so scary when I imagined what it did to people in the movies.

Then my father wrote a letter to the Kenyan police informing them about what had happened in the night and what he had found. We were all convinced that they would do something about it. After he completed the letter, he took it with the bullet together to the police headquarters in the district.

They took it and they asked my dad to go and my dad left. In the Kakuma refugee camp most of the police personnel were from the Turkana region. We believed they were all connected to those who threatened the refugees because most of the high-ranking officers were from the same regions.

This made it very hard for most of the refugees to deal with the local police who were supposed to be friendly with them.

Chapter 6

The Kakuma Refugee camp is situated in the second poorest region in Kenya and as a result of this poverty, there are ongoing tensions between the refugees and the local community that has occasionally resulted in violence.

Compared to the wider region, the Kakuma camp has better health facilities and a higher percentage of children in full-time education, which often results in a general perception that the refugees were better off than the locals.

The host community is composed largely of nomadic pastoralists who stick to their traditions and don't co-operate with refugees. The camp however is becoming a normal part of the regional socio-economic landscape and a part of the livelihood options available in the region for locals themselves as mentioned earlier.

Kakuma is one of two largest refugee camps in Kenya, second to the Dadaab Refugee Camp in the East. Malnutrition, communicable disease outbreaks and malaria were all ongoing problems as donor support has faltered due to conflicts in other parts of the world according to the UNHCR administration in the region.

Many people in Kakuma were long-term refugees living in hopelessness and desperation. Some were born there and grew up there knowing nowhere other than Kakuma and the situation is particularly bad for young people who have never seen any other part of the world that they live in. Many of them hope to leave Kakuma for a third country for resettlement in another part of the world but this isn't and often will not happen for most of them. The

The Reflection of my Journey to the Republic of South Sudan

highest on the wish list was to get a chance to go an OECD country. For example, the Lost Boys of the Sudan were the first group of young people who were very lucky to be resettled in the United States, Australia, New Zealand and Canada.

During our times in Kakuma one thing I would not forget is when we used to go for a distance of two hours every day to fetch water and painfully carried twenty litres of water or more in 45 degrees Celsius temperatures. This kind of hard work even made our life harder. Our parents assigned it to us as our duty. We saw it as a hard, heavy job and if we refused to do it we were punished by them or our uncles so we had to avoid punishment by doing what we were asked to do. It was a daily full-time job for us kids.

One day my cousins Atong, Amuor, Aluel, Akech and I woke up early in the morning and went to the river in Kakuma where we could fetch water. When we arrived there, we started digging on the riverbank where we always got clean water. Suddenly a Turkana man appeared with an AK47 machine gun and we became terrified thinking that they would shoot us as they did before in our compound. This was how difficult life was in Kakuma especially for children like us. We were not sure of what was in his mind. We screamed and started running and luckily, he didn't shoot at us but we were extremely scared. Our existence was in danger from all angles and we thought we would never find happiness in our lives. It was everyone's wish in the refugee camp that one day we would have better lives once we were outside the refugee camp. However, that wasn't always the case and that will be reflected in my life in Melbourne, Australia. Only a few were lucky to go to the United States and other parts of the western world.

The Kakuma Refugee Camp wasn't associated only with those I mentioned. We as the Sudanese were our own problem among ourselves. I could remember very well that there was heavy fighting between three tribes: the Nuer, Dinka and Equartorian people in the camp. The Nuer community were fighting against the Dinka and that fight cost many lives including my two uncles who were living with us in our compound. It was a very sad year for us. I was very young— about eleven. I could even see elders from Dinka tribes holding sticks, shields and spears. Some could even have more than five spears in their hands running around everywhere going to fight.

As a result, many people started panicking and ran to the UNHCR compound for protection but the Kenyan police personnel were employed around the compound to not allow people in and started shooting directly into crowd when you pushed in aggressively. It was an order from the UN security protection unit. People were scared including myself, however, my father who is a great man looked after us very well. He took us to a safe place away from the fighting zone —one of his Ethiopian friends' house.

On our way we saw a lot of Kenyan police vehicles on the road everywhere with guns and they looked very scary. My father was holding my hand so I could not run away because I was crying too much and my body was shaking a lot.

Before we could get to my dad's friend house, the fight was about to break out again in the UN compound between the Nuer and Dinka communities, but luckily the Kenyan police came in and beat up everyone with sticks which eventually broke up the fight and separated these two communities. After that they just sat opposite each other glaring at each other without any further moves thanks to the scary Kenyan police.

The fighting lasted for nearly three months. We lost many great young men during this unnecessary fighting. I can still remember seeing dead bodies lying on streets and open spaces on our way to the UN compound. My father covered my eyes with his hand so that I would not keep staring at them, but I had already seen them. I couldn't sleep properly that day. It was my first time seeing a person lying dead in an open place—it was terrible.

The second terrible and memorable thing I saw was seeing people moving with their belongings everyday carrying their clothes and small children, I didn't like it at all. It was a really sad sight. Kenyan police drove around everywhere day and night preventing and stopping the fighting. They really did very well in that regard.

That was my life experience of hearing gunshots and seeing dead bodies on the ground in the Kakuma Refugee Camp. After all the fighting subsided, fear remained and the people were still scared. It took almost another three months for life to return to normal. It was a great deal for everybody in the camp including the Dinkas and Nuers. After three months people started slowly to do normal activities and started to go back to schools, but still those who lost loved ones, during the fighting never felt at ease. They still feel sad about it including myself and my family. We will never see my two uncles; they are gone for good.

No one ever feels proud of communal fights whether you won or lost. When you win you still lose lives the same as when you lose war you still lose lives. You will never be proud. War is sometimes an evil.

When I go to bed and think about it, especially the intercommunal fighting of Kakuma, I cry inside my heart and eventually tears flow from my eyes unintended. The writing of this story of the Kakuma Refugee Camp reminds me a lot of good and sad stories of my life there that I will never forget. I wrote this story in Melbourne, Australia in a beautiful area known as Elwood Beach.

There are a lot of good memories to remember about Kakuma Refugee Camp and a lot of bad stories as well.

One year later heavy fighting broke out again between the Dinka community and the Equartorian community. The same thing happened again and many lives were lost. It was like a repetition of a curse. There was death everywhere we went and it kept following us. First from the Sudan to Ethiopia then from Ethiopia back to the Sudan and again on the way to Kenya and again in Kakuma Refugee Camp in Kenya. Everywhere we went there was a war and death.

Things weren't really good in the camp despite the constant presence of the Kenyan police. There were three fights in a short period of time. In fact, they made life even harder for many refugees who were in the camp. It was like living in a war zone of the Sudan.

Chapter 7

The Nuer community fought with the Dinka community. The Equartorian community fought with the Dinka community and the Dinka community fought within itself. The Dinka community and other refugee communities also fought a lot with the local community, the Turkana. At this point fighting in the camp became useless and mad no sense at all and just complicated life badly in the camp. I would like to say R.I.P to those who died during all of those fighting and those lives lost in the journey from South Sudan to Ethiopia to refugee camp in Kenya. Please while you are reading this book just observe one minute of silence for them and say R.I.P to all of them. They are our brothers; sisters and they are all human beings like us and we will never forget them. All those fights brought a lot of shame and problems in our communities including tribalism.

There were some unpreventable deaths too. One night, our neighbor's daughter went out to a pit toilet in her compound which was outside her hut, at the sharp corner of her compound's fence. It was either on her way back to the hut or before she could even reach it. No one exactly knows how it happened. She was fatally shot right in her chest and died instantly. No one went outside as people were not aware that there was someone outside till morning. In the morning she was found lying dead, with no explanation nothing, just left to be buried. The finger was only being pointed at Turkana bandits as there was no one in possession of guns in camp among refugees except them. People

Kenya and Kakuma Refugee Camp 1990–2005

in the camp were so scared to go out of their huts in the night to see what was happening.

She was one of our family friends and we knew her very well. She was a very respectful young girl and everyone was affected by her death. That was another way we lost our community members.

The constant death among us was a great concern and great deal. It worried us a lot so praying to God was the only option left for us. Even we children became regular night prayers attendees in the Church. We went to church at around eight pm and finished at around nine pm or later. The aim of regular prayers was to lament and ask God to bring peace to our homeland, South Sudan, so that we could go back home. It was a great deal and I could even see women and men alike crying while praying in church. I even shed tears as well for the fact that their prayers touched me too.

As a child, Kakuma Christmas time was the best time of every year. Seeing people marching on the road and the army and police singing church songs and people of all ages wearing black and white. I will never forget it.

While living there in Kakuma Refugee Camp, two of my sisters got sick and died young. I couldn't understand what disease killed them because I was still too young. The only thing I could clearly see was them being buried near the Kakuma Town graveyard and this prompted me to constantly ask my parents whether my sisters would come back again. I didn't know the meaning of death until I grew up and became more aware. I could only hope they rest in peace. It became one of the things that made me not forget life in the Kakuma Refugee Camp.

My step mum used to go to the Kakuma main hospital with me to pray for the sick because she was a church woman and that was their duty as a member of the church leadership, the pastoral care group. Everything was complicated and it wasn't an easy life after all. I took it this way: Life is very complicated you never know

The Reflection of my Journey to the Republic of South Sudan

where it will end. You can have a good life today and tomorrow you may end up having a bad life. So, life is very confusing. Just focus on what's important in your life.

Chapter 8

I view life as a journey. A journey that may unexpectedly be short or long. Some die young, some get old and some are unborn. Life is unfinished business.

What is life but unfinished business? We are all powerless to undo the past, but the future is up to us by making the present through our thoughts and actions. We are bound by the past, but at every moment we sometimes exercise a certain amount of free will and choices and make the future what we will timely enjoy or regret. The surest way to make this pleasant and profitable journey each day and to the highest of our knowledge, or to the best of our ability, is to avoid doing the things which will handicap us in the future. In other words, do not allow an action that will lead to a failure as that will result in painful unfinished business.

What is life but unfinished business? It is the worries and complaints you have about not having enough time to do your favorite things before the end. Unfinished business is not just the story of how and why and when you decided to tie up the loose ending. It's also about the extraordinary and unexpected events that would unfold once you embark on the journey toward completion. This is an uplifting and true-life story I have been through.

What is life but unfinished business again? It is a rich, wise and powerful work that reminds us to be mindful of what is truly important in our journey of life. Unfinished business defines what was carried over by you from the past and we will take with us into the future whatever remains undone.

The Reflection of my Journey to the Republic of South Sudan

I used to admire 50 Cent's theory of "Get Rich or Die Trying". But there is much more to life. Life needs more: life requires money, food, water, shelters, etc. And most of all spiritually life requires God and love for one another. Nobody can ever say they have fully accomplished life. Not even billionaires. Life is unaccomplished.

The statistics of the world are just an example: an approximated 99.9% of the world's population are living under the poverty line and consider themselves as poor under the theory of "die trying". Meanwhile, only 0.1% of the entire world's population lives under the theory of "Get Rich" but that doesn't mean their satisfaction is fulfilled.

No matter what your journey looks like, I strongly believe that God has created a new day for every one of us, to live in community, to laugh and cry, to hurt and to celebrate with each other. No matter what is happening throughout your journey, whether the transformation is tough, or whether life doesn't always end up where we think we will. We have to remember that life is a struggle, a progress and filled with purpose and passion. And the best part of the journey is that the God of the Universe sometimes allows us to play a part in changing the world. Isn't that a trip? Yes, it is.

Finally, the beauty of life is what you make of your journey. No matter what, you're going to mess up sometimes. It's a universal truth. Just because you fail once, doesn't mean you're going to fail at everything or all the times. Keep trying, hold on, and always, always, always believe in yourself. Because if you don't, then who will? So, keep your head high, keep your chin up. And most importantly, keep smiling, because life's a beautiful thing and there's so much to smile about and so little accomplishment from it.

People change. Time's moving. Years go by and this, or that, is exactly the definition of life as a journey. My advice to you is to never laugh at a poor person or make a joke —help them if you have something to help them with to make them enjoy the world as well.

Chapter 9

When I was living in Kakuma Refugee Camp I always had a dream of helping poor people in my lifetime, but I was young and poor too. I didn't have anything at all, but I believed one day God would help me and I would help a poor person in my life. I always put the divine God first in everything I plan to do.

I feel sad seeing a poor person, especially a disabled person or someone I heard had lost a mother or father and it hurts me a lot when hearing it narrated. I always like to ask a person if his or her parents are alive. I feel hurt a lot when I heard that they are all dead or they are poor, I never worried about myself but them, the poor, especially when hearing their sad stories.

My daily prayers to God ask him to give me the power to help a poor person. I just want to raise up a poor person whether he/she is white or black. I just want to help them and I want to show them my love. I don't want to die and leave this world without helping a poor person.

I am always afraid of death. This is my daily golden dream and I strongly believe in myself that I will achieve it one day. I always put God first in every step I take and I understand the meaning of importance of helping others.

I was helped by the United Nations High Commissioner for Refugees (UNHCR) for 13 years of my life living in the Kakuma Refugee Camp. Without them I would have not been alive today.

It is a dusty land, a land of dry rivers surrounded by acacia trees and red mountains. A camp where there is no electricity and

The Reflection of my Journey to the Republic of South Sudan

no public transport. This camp is home to over 80,000 refugees, three quarters of whom are South Sudanese and the rest from other devastated countries, such as Somalia, Uganda, Burundi, Ethiopia, and Rwanda. 86 % are school aged children but most are orphans.

Every Christmas Day, you could hear the sound of singing, drummers and chanting of Jesus' name before you can see the crowd. The South Sudanese Churches at the Kakuma Refugee Camp would march in the streets celebrating Christmas. The Kakuma Camp is divided into six zones which are determined and dominated by the protestant parishes as follows: Zone 1 is the Episcopal Church of South Sudan; Zone 2 is the Episcopal Church of South Sudan; Zone 3 is the Episcopal Church of South Sudan; Zone 4 is the Anglican Church of South Sudan; Zone 4 is the Episcopal Church of South Sudan; Zone 5 is the Baptist Church of South Sudan; and, Zone 6 is the Episcopal Church of South Sudan.

Growing up in the Kakuma Refugee Camp was not easy at all and it was a very hard life. When we were kids in Kakuma we could be beaten for any of the following reasons:

1. Crying after being beaten
2. Not crying
3. Crying without being beaten
4. Standing while the elders were seated
5. Sitting while the elders stood
6. Walking around aimlessly where the elders were seated
7. Talking back to an elder
8. Not replying to an elder
9. Spending too much time without being beaten
10. Singing after being admonished
11. Not greeting visitors
12. Eating food prepared for the visitors
13. Crying to go with the visitors when the visitors were leaving

Kenya and Kakuma Refugee Camp 1990–2005

14. Refusing to eat
15. Coming back home after sunset
16. Eating at a neighbour's home
17. Generally being moody
18. Generally being too excited
19. Fighting with your age mate and losing
20. Fighting with your age mate and winning
21. Eating too slowly
22. Eating too quickly
23. Eating too much
24. Sleeping while the elders were already awake
25. Looking at the visitors while they were eating
26. Stumbling and falling when walking

These things made our life difficult and complicated. I grew up in environment where the elders disciplined us with sticks. It was another way to teach us so we could be great leaders in future. Without all of this I couldn't be the person I am today. It made me feel stronger and able to pass through all hardships.

Chapter 10

In 2005, God did open doors for many South Sudanese from Kakuma to go settle in countries like Australia, Canada and the USA. My family and I ended up in Melbourne, Australia after passing all the pre-requisites.

We left the Kakuma Refugee camp in June on a bus for Nairobi, Kenya where we caught a flight to Australia. It was the happiest day of our lives and it was a moment of realization of a change we had been wishing for, for a very long time. It was the day when our dreams of success were fulfilled and it was so wonderful.

I didn't know what Australia looked like but I had heard about it from my cousins who had come here before us and told us that it was a great country. On our way to Nairobi by bus through several towns I saw a lot of interesting things which were very rarely seen in camp, such as large shops, people selling roadside fruits such as bananas, mangoes, etc. and clothes and many other things. We also saw some of the Kenyan police at checkpoints with guns which was intimidating. They kept stopping our bus and asked everyone to get out of the bus and asked a lot of questions and demanded bribes or else.

They pulled out our driver at every checkpoint and asked him for his driving license and money. In Kenya, many police officers including those who are high ranking, will ask for kidogido or bribes. They will also take money from passengers whether you have the documents you want or not. No matter how well prepared you are, a Kenyan police officer could still ask for kidogido.

Kenya and Kakuma Refugee Camp 1990–2005

My brother Manyang's skill of speaking both the languages of Kiswahili and English very well was an advantage for us compared to those who spoke neither of them. When we reached every checkpoint, he got off and started talking to them and started with a greeting and introduction of who he was because he was a Kenyan Boy Scouts member. He was also wearing his scout's uniform as proof as the Boy Scouts were well respected in Kenya.

The journey to Nairobi was too long and it was almost fifteen hours of sitting in one place. The road was not very good there too and there were a lot of car accidents. Bad driving also contributed as drivers drove very fast despite the condition of the road.

I was scared and nervous seeing Kenyan police with guns everywhere. It wasn't safe for me at all and I didn't enjoy that journey at all because of the police.

After this long journey we arrived in Nairobi, Kenya in the late afternoon of the next day and were picked up by my uncle daughter Atong Kuol Manyang and my older sister Atong Malet Manyang. It was the first time in my entire life that I saw tall buildings and felt cold weather as I used to live in a mud hut in Kakuma in 45 degree temperatures every day.

I started to realise that I was out of Kakuma finally, out from it going to a new country to start a new life. I got away from the Turkana people, from the Kenyan police and away from all those threats to my life in the refugee camp but I was also worried about people that we left behind in Kakuma including my childhood friends and the rest of my family members.

In less than two hours after our arrival to where my sister and cousin lived, we ate, dressed up and we got back into a car direct to the Nairobi International Airport. We left our younger brother Guem Malet crying inside the house as he was too sad seeing us leaving him behind and heading to somewhere that he didn't understand.

The Reflection of my Journey to the Republic of South Sudan

My family was separated in two for our interviews to go to Australia. My brothers Guem Malet Manyang, Thon Malet Manyang, Atong Malet Manyang, my mother Abuk Chagai and my father Malet Manyang were interviewed together and did not pass. But I had applied with my stepmother, brother, my stepbrothers and one of my stepsisters and we were approved and passed our interview so we got to leave to Australia and the family had to be separated.

It was the first time in my life that I saw Nairobi Airport with its big planes. We lined up and our travel documents were checked by airport security. After general checking, our names were called out and then we boarded a plane. I was so excited and felt very happy but I was still worried about my family left behind in the camp and in Nairobi.

It was like a dream. Up in the air, I couldn't believe it: I had left Kenya. The journey from the Nairobi International Airport to Dubai was still too long in some sense. On June 30th 2005 we arrived in Melbourne, Australia, where the weather was freezing, but we managed to survive it.

After ten years in Australia I was able to get Australian citizenship and an Australian passport which encouraged me to travel to South Sudan for the first time in my entire life. And that is where I reflected on my journey to South Sudan.

PART TWO

Melbourne, Australia

2005 – 2015

Chapter 11

My life in Melbourne

After enduring a long flight and the cold Melbourne winter, we settled and started navigating our lives in the new country and environment. As a young man, I started going to nightclubs in 2008.

Some of the South Sudanese girls and boys whom I used to go to nightclubs with now have established their own families, some have five kids or more, some are single like myself, and some became alcoholic and drug addicts. Some have confused lives they don't even know how to get out of. Some of them end up in prison as criminals. A majority of them never settled and even today still attend nightclubs.

I know in reading this you will be asking where I am now and what I am doing. Well I did eventually stop going to nightclubs and the reason I stopped partying was because of the kids that I used to see going to school.

Some of them became worse moving on to committing multiple crimes. My generation moved on and new eighteen-year olds emerged and were repeating the same mistakes of our generation.

During my nightclubbing days, my stepmother never wanted me to go out in any circumstance. She always talked to me but I didn't take her advice. I always ignored her and opened the door myself and left. I just wanted to go and meet up with my friends and party. I would travel long distances around Melbourne and Victoria, and even interstate just to party. I found it exciting and interesting because I was young and naive. I didn't even know whether I would grow out of it but finally I stopped partying.

I woke up one day and I realised I wanted to focus on my life and help others as it had been in my mind since Kakuma. Eventually my stepmother who always talked to me didn't give up on me. She was happy because I never brought problems on myself or my family. I grew up amongst elders and young people which was handy for me. The young people including myself took their parents and elders as their enemies rather than their advisers and guardians. I thought this was the reason why some young people ended up committing a multitude of crimes. They refused to listen to their parents and elders.

Listening to our parents and elders prepares us to be great people. Taking your mother and your father as your friends makes better and stronger relationships and friendships. Trusting them will let them trust you too.

When I used to go to the nightclub, my father would call me on the phone while I was in the club and advise me to take precautions. His words of advice were very powerful and I always considered them while dancing and playing. I always listened to him and to other elders.

One thing I used to be so scared of was the police presence. When people started fighting in the club, the police were always outside ready to stop any fight. Who knows what they would use when they enter the club. I never stopped watching a fight. I always left the scene and stood far away from the real fighting spot. I always didn't want to be involved with the police officers' job unless they knew I was helping them. The reason was that I was scared to be involved in somebody else's problem and end up getting a criminal record unnecessarily.

When I look back now at our time comparing it with the current teenagers, I can see a lot of difference between us. We were better

Melbourne, Australia 2005–2015

behaved I believe, but also the laws weren't as strict as they are today. Police officers sometimes are friendly to the general public, but not always.

In life, people often try to tell you what to do. Mostly they base their advice on what they have experienced. Sometimes it is based on what they wish they could have done in their time. Most often it might be out of love for you. So my advice is that there is no need to be angry toward them. You're the one who will live with any of your decisions.

If you are being pushed to go to college, it is for you not for them. You can be a lawyer or police officer if you want to but your parents or relatives need you to go school till you realize your dream career.

We should listen to others especially elders and our parents, but not let our anyone that we do not trust wants the best for us make decisions for us. If you don't want to go to college, there are plenty of trade schools, apprenticeships, and many other education pathways available. You can join any of them and life goes on. College always be there for you though if you wish. Follow your heart and do whatever you think is better for you but within the law. Stay away from criminal activities and you will be fine.

Be honest to your friends, your enemies, your parents and most importantly to yourself. If you have the slightest hesitation about your actions or words, think twice and find a better way in which it won't be offensive. When you look at yourself in the mirror, in your mind you want to be proud of yourself and the choices you have made. That won't be the case if you're not brutally honest with yourself. A true man takes the consequences of his actions and doesn't try to get out of them or pretend that they didn't happen. If you make a mistake, admit it and make it right. It's always better to correct yourself of the mistakes you committed. You always have to be answerable to yourself in the mirror.

The Reflection of my Journey to the Republic of South Sudan

All job providers in Australia now go through a police record check and if you have any criminal record you will suffer a lot and you won't get the job you want. The best way to avoid it is to stay away from crimes.

Chapter 12

On a Saturday night I went out with my friends to a nightclub in the Melbourne CBD. That night, I cannot exactly remember the date, but I do remember it was August.

It was a warm night and my friends headed to a nightclub on McKillop Street. The night started very well but ended badly for me. This was the first time in my entire club life that I found myself in trouble. While in the nightclub one South Sudanese person who was a well-known DJ asked me politely if I could stand at the door and collect the entry fee along with his girlfriend. I agreed and I let my friends go inside the club then remained outside standing closer to the security guards at the entry.

Around 2am, a lot of people entered and the party started while I still collected money at the nightclub entry. Meanwhile, my friends started drinking alcohol heavily inside the club. They apparently became annoying to other people inside. They started a fight with another group of people inside. I was still outside at the door collecting money. One of the security guards who saw me with them on our arrival ran outside and asked if could be of any help to stop the fight. I rushed inside and I saw them fighting on the dance floor. Everyone was paying attention to the fighting and the girls were screaming loudly.

The fight went on for almost half an hour inside the club. I pulled out some of my friends and told them that I am very sad with them. Luckily, they listened to me and the DJ stopped the music. Everyone started to leave. The police were called by one of

The Reflection of my Journey to the Republic of South Sudan

the security guards outside with us. Outside, the fight started again between the girls who were involved in the initial fight inside. The fighting became out of control.

The police started arriving and begin to arrest some of them including two of my friends. That night was the worst ever night: things turned out very ugly and bad. My friends who were arrested started swearing at the police officers.

I asked one of the leading senior constables if I could talk to them to calm them down and he allowed me to do so. While I was talking to them a sergeant in charge of that unit came out of nowhere and he pointed his finger at me and started yelling at me.

I looked at him and was about to explain myself to him but he was out of control with his anger and charged toward me. He asked me to move away but while I was leaving, he kept following me with aggressive behavior. When I went further away and stood, he came again and told me to leave the entire area.

I was still thinking that talking to him and explaining what had happened in the nightclub would help calm him down but he didn't want to listen. Instead he ordered his unit to arrest me. At least five of them jumped on me and pushed me onto the ground and dragged me. On the floor they all put their hands and knees on me spreading me out flat. I couldn't breathe properly and my body was in pain. They handcuffed my wrists causing a lot of extra pain. I wanted to scream but I could not make any voice.

Everyone was just looking at me and wondering why I was arrested. Some were even in shock to see me as the one being arrested because some were thinking that I was working with them. I heard one of the South Sudanese young men telling the police officers that this young man you guys arrested is working with the Victoria Police and the Salvation Army.

The police officers couldn't believe that I worked for the Victoria Police. In fact I was working as a multicultural crimes stopper in the Sunshine area. I was being used to bridge the gap between African youths and Victoria Police members in the Sunshine area. The sergeant continued to be rude and racist to many other African youths at the nightclub.

On the same night the police officers took me to my residential address at Ascot Vale and they returned my wallet and belt. I limped inside my house in the presence of my friend Chol Akech whom I shared a house with. He had been sleeping inside at the time and hadn't gone out with me.

It was five am when I arrived home. I tried to take my clothes off, but realised I couldn't do it. My whole body was aching, however, there wasn't an alternative. In the end I managed to get them off anyway but with a lot of pain. I could see bruises on my knees and my elbows and all over my body.

My stepbrother Marin called me to check whether I was being released or not because he had been present at the nightclub when the incident took place. Then I told him that the police had dropped me to my house and I was fine which wasn't true.

I was saying that to not let him worry too much about me. I was not feeling well at all that night and I was so sad for them and myself and my body was so weak and sore. Three weeks later I received a letter in my mailbox requesting me to go to Magistrate Court in the city.

It was a great shock to me. Before my court date I received a phone call from Sergeant Matt and Mr Gilbert to go to the Sunshine Police Station to meet them. I was concerned believing that this was getting serious.

When I arrived, I realised that Chris is a very respectful man and Matt is now a good friend of mine. They questioned me about what had happened to me in the city at the nightclub. I put my head down and explained the whole scenario and how it went wrong. Before I visited them at the Sunshine Police Station, I made some inquiries on what I should say and I was told that I would have to take my court papers with me so I did.

In our meeting before the court date, they gave me some ideas on how to begin a new life here in Australia after this case. They also helped me a lot on what to expect at my hearing date at the magistrate's court. Things like before entering a courtroom I would pass through a security gate. I would be asked to take out my belt and wallet and anything else in my pockets as well. It was my first in court and I was feeling very nervous about it.

After meeting with these two important police officers, I walked over to the legal services next door and asked them if they could represent me on my hearing day. They took all my papers and I was taken to an interview room so that I could provide them all the necessary information. After the interview they agreed and told me yes, they would represent me in court. I was relieved after their response because I was so scared since I didn't know what the judge's decision would be and how to respond to it.

I was also well supported by different individuals before I attended court. I collected six support letters from friends who worked in Victoria Police plus a letter from the Salvation Army's former coordinator Lauren Cockerel and my own apology letter. I wrote an apology letter to the magistrate court as I knew it would mean a lot to them and it would show that I was a responsible person. Indeed, I believed the letters influenced the outcome a lot in court.

I thought the judge was very overwhelmed by reading them. Minutes after he read my support letters, he asked me to get up and to explain myself. I proceeded to do so and he asked me what I was doing for a living. For me it was a great opportunity, so I told him about the volunteering work I have been doing with Salvation Army youth street team. He was interested to hear more about it and I went further explaining it with confidence.

Melbourne, Australia 2005–2015

He then gave me papers to enroll in an anger management course and to pay three hundred dollars to the Beyond Blue charity organization for good behaviour. I left the magistrate court an unsatisfied young man but I never shared it with my family or friends even though I wasn't heavily fined. I was charged to complete a division program on April 22nd 2014 for the offence(s) of:

1. Contravene Decision Given to move on
2. Hinder Police
3. Resist police
4. Refuse to State Name/ Address.

I wasn't convinced at all of the validity of the charges. I was given three weeks to do the following orders. I was also asked to provide court with a receipt of payment from the organisation that I was referred to or provide a money order/ cheque to the court made payable to a specific agency that would train me after I completed an anger management course then provide a copy of the certificate of completion to the court before mid October 2014.

This course also was a part of the good behavior bond/ punishment for the duration of one year.

It took me a long time to complete the court order as required by the Magistrate and that was considered a violation, but it wasn't as I had moved to Colac town to work in the meat factory. I wasn't doing it out of the blue and informed the Magistrate Court to let them know that I worked five days a week in Colac which was quite a distance away from the course provider. The court did accept my request. The case was still pending on my record even though I had paid the three hundred Australian dollars to Beyond Blue.

In August 2014 I moved back to Melbourne to organise my travel to South Sudan for December 2014. I sent a letter via email

The Reflection of my Journey to the Republic of South Sudan

to the Magistrate Court to let them know that I would be away for a very long time. I told them in the letter that when I returned from South Sudan, I would complete my court orders. They didn't reply to my email so two days later I went to the Magistrate Court in person and enquired whether they had received my email.

They said yes, and that they had received it and my heart began to pound for I was worried that they would not let me travel to South Sudan as I had planned. However, they gave me the green light to leave the country if I wanted to.

PART THREE

South Sudan

2015 – 2017

Chapter 13

A journey of a thousand miles began with a single step. In the middle of 2014, I had made up my mind to travel to my motherland South Sudan. This was to be the very first time in my life that I would see South Sudan. Before December 2014 I had started to share my willingness to go to South Sudan with my friends and family. All of them were happy and encouraged me to go there and some of them said that they were going to miss me.

On Tuesday, the 16th of December at ten am my friend Chol Akech drove me to Melbourne International Airport. After I had checked in, Chol said goodbye to me and he left to go back home. I was at the gate sitting on the chair feeling very happy. I couldn't wait to reach to South Sudan to see my family and friends that I hadn't seen for many years. I had been away from them for such a long time.

After our airline gate opened, we lined up to board the plane. It was a long journey; a thirteen-hour direct flight from Melbourne to Dubai. I was very tired from sitting in one place for so many hours. One of the flight attendants walked toward me with a smiling face and asked me if I was feeling ok in my seat. I told her my knees were hurting and that the seat was annoying me badly. She told me to get up and come with her. I got up and I took all my belongings and followed her to a seat in the front row and she told me to sit there.

I sat down and stretched my feet. I felt very comfortable on that seat. I thanked her. While in the plane I took out the book 'The

The Reflection of my Journey to the Republic of South Sudan

White Masai' to read and I was reading it with great enjoyment and it made my journey feel much shorter.

I was just imagining what South Sudan was going to look like as I had heard a lot of stories about it and read about it on the internet. I couldn't wait to reach there so I could see my motherland and my family and friends that I hadn't seen for many years. I had been away from them and I had not met them in person my entire life. It seemed like the plane was not moving fast at all and I wanted to get there really quickly.

One of the passengers who was sitting next to me was a business man who traveling to Dubai. He was a nice person as I observed from the way he was talking to me. He asked me my name and I told him and he then asked about my nationality. I told him proudly that I was a South Sudanese. He showed more interest in talking to me. We had a very nice conversation. We continued talking and he told me his whole life story. Unfortunately, I don't remember his name but he certainly seemed to be a very nice person. We shook hands after our conversation and I fell asleep.

I had been very tired when I left Melbourne with not much sleep. My previous five days had been spent well with my friends and family members in Melbourne. I slept in the plane for a couple of hours.

Around ten am the announcement came from one of the flight attendants that we were going to land in Dubai International Airport soon and everyone should wake up and prepare themselves and put on their seatbelts. We landed safely.

The journey was too long and my feet and body were very tired. Dubai looked very nice and clean. It was a nice place; the sun was shining and it was really warm outside.

While in Dubai I walked towards the transit area. I walked toward the notice board area to check for my next flight to Juba in South Sudan. It was an eight hour long wait.

I was so tired I couldn't feel my body at all; as if it wasn't mine. After I checked my next flight I came back and lay down on two chairs very tired and with a headache at the same time.

The hours passed and I woke up and I walked toward the departure counter, took out my passport and gave it to one of the staff. I was asked to provide a South Sudanese I.D or passport. I told them it was my first time going to South Sudan and that I had never been there before. I told them I grown up in the refugee camp in Northern Kenya and that I had never been to South Sudan. The lady checking my passport went and called her manager and I was pulled out of the line and to the side and the line continued.

I was very worried about it. The manager came and asked me the same question. I gave him the same reply. I saw my uncle Panther Mayen Leek in the Dubai Airport traveling to South Sudan as well. He walked towards me and asked what happened and why I was standing here. I explained it to him and he told me I would be ok and not to worry about it. Then he said that he would see me inside the plane.

The manager came back with his worker holding my Australian passport in his hand and asked me if I could call anyone at the Juba International Airport. I told him that I didn't know the direct number of the Juba International Airport or anyone there. After this my passport was stamped with my ticket and returned back to me. A security officer apologised to me and wished me a safe journey to my motherland South Sudan.

There were many people I knew traveling to South Sudan from Dubai. It was the last destination with only five hours to go to South Sudan. Before the plane took off the pilot and his crew were getting ready, I saw one South Sudanese young boy and his mother sitting in different seats.

The boy was sitting near me before plane took off and he started asking me a few questions about South Sudan and I told him it's my first time going to South Sudan and that I had never been there before. He was very shocked and he continued to ask a lot of questions. His mother turned around from the front seat to tell him to stop annoying me. I told her it was ok, and to let him talk, and that I was enjoying it. She said ok and we continued our talk.

He told me that he had heard that South Sudan was the dangerous place.

"Is that true?" I asked him. "You know, it's going to be ok, don't worry about what people's told you about it."

He thanked me. About half an hour later we were served with food. I felt Dubai airlines had great service and that the staff looked happy and friendly to the passengers helping all that asked and speaking nicely. In the plane one passenger unfortunately was vomiting. I asked him if he was ok and he said he was and that he would be ok. At 2:30 pm we landed safely at Juba International airport.

Before we departed the plane, I could see that the weather outside seemed very hot. I was feeling tired again and the passengers were exiting slowly. I couldn't wait and was anxious to move as quick as I could to meet with my father and relatives that I had missed for many years.

Finally, we got outside and the high temperature hit me. It was too hot, 40 degrees, and I took off my suit jacket as I was sweating profusely. Outside the plane I knelt down and kissed the ground of my motherland South Sudan and gave one minute of silence for the people who had died during the civil war between the North and South. With tears trickling down my face, other people looked at me as if I was crazy.

One of the passengers came and held my arm saying to take it easy and he welcomed me to South Sudan with a happy voice. I wiped tears from my eyes and I shook his hand and told him thanks brother and he left. I saw my father who was standing in the airport waiting area waiting for me. I ran towards him with more tears in my eyes. I gave him a big hug holding him for a few minutes. I was so happy seeing him again after many years apart and to be in my motherland South Sudan for the first time.

My father took me to his office nearby as he worked at the airport. His office was very nice with air conditioning. I sat on the chair of my father while he got me cold water. After half an hour we left his office to go home.

My father was driving his car along roads in Juba that were far too busy. It was hard for a driver to give way to another driver, as motorcycles and cars were squashed together on the roads and my dad was driving very carefully.

My father the driver got us safely to the home of my uncle's daughter, Achol Aborish. She saw me and screamed very loudly calling my name. She was very happy and I was very happy to see her. She gave me a hug along with the rest of the family. My sister Achol got me a chair and stopped what she was doing to come and sit next to me.

All my family were very happy to see me of course and I was feeling the same way. I was surrounded by my family and all were asking me about Australia and life there. I told them about it. My sister Achol went to the local shop and bought me coca cola and a bottle of cold water.

A few minutes later I put water in a bucket and took it to a bathroom to have shower. The water was too cold but nice. The temperature outside was too hot and after the shower I felt very good. My body was still very tired.

I was shown inside where I could sleep in the house that was made out of mud. The mud hut inside was very hot too and I opened all the windows so air could come inside. The air coming in was hot but I couldn't feel it because I was so tired from the long journey.

The Reflection of my Journey to the Republic of South Sudan

I slept until eight pm waking up to go outside to sit around a table talking to my father. I loved listening to the radio a lot and hearing news from it since the TV was not common over there. The TV was inside his room but it felt very hot to be inside so we relaxed outside until around ten or eleven pm. We then retired to sleep.

Some people were outside but it's too dangerous to stay out long as Juba in South Sudan is not safe at all. Gunshots happen every night. Criminals would walk around at night, sometimes stealing from properties. The theft of mobile phones, iPads, computers or money was common and often people were killed even if they had nothing on them. Every night we heard gunshots in our area.

We used to live near the army barracks and our house was surrounded by soldiers but it was still very dangerous. Killing had become very easy and simple in South Sudan. Often as simple as drinking water. People never walk freely at night.

A few weeks later in South Sudan on Saturday night I asked my father if I could go to a nightclub in Juba. My father remained silent. Without saying anything about it I couldn't asked him again because I knew he was not happy with this request. Later he asked me who would take me to a nightclub. I told him I would go with Thon my older brother. My father told me to call him, I took out my phone and I made the call.

Thon lives a bit further away from our area. My brother Thon turned up about an hour later and my father got up and went inside his room to bring out his car key. He gave it to Thon asking him to take me to a nightclub. I was very happy and I went inside to change my clothes. I dressed up nicely and we left heading out to a nightclub.

My brother Thon Malet was driving and ten minutes later on our way to the club we saw soldiers and police working the nightshift wearing their uniforms and carrying AK47s. Close to them was a checkpoint area where they stopped our car and asked my brother where we were going at this time of night.

My brother told them that we were going home. He was lying to them because if he told them that we were going to a nightclub they would have beaten us up and called us criminals. Or told us to go back home. So he had no choice but to tell them that we were going home. I was scared seeing the guns and they looked very scary too. They told us to get out of the car. There were four of us inside the car and we did as we were told. They started to search inside the car for guns or any dangerous equipment.

Naturally we had no contraband. We were told to raise our hands and we did so. They searched us for the possibility of pistols on us. We could hear gunshot sounds but it was far away. The officer told us to get back into our car and said to us drive careful because soldiers and police were everywhere blocking most roads. If my brother drove fast, they might shoot first and question later. Brother Thon drove slowly and turned off music inside the car and put his window down so he could hear it if any soldier said stop. We continued driving until we reach the nightclub named "Signature".

It was one of the famous clubs in Juba. We saw everyone standing outside getting ready to go inside. I saw police officers carrying guns in the nightclub working as security. In the club I did not feel safe or happy with people carrying guns everywhere in South Sudan. After we got into line and paid our entry money we were admitted inside.

The music was very nice. People were dancing crazily and enjoying the club very much. I saw one of my childhood friends that I had not seen for many years inside the club. I walked towards him and asked him "Do you remember me?" With a big smile he said "No but I don't remember you. Tell me your name!"

Then he remembered me and he told me that I looked different. "You are a big man tall and huge." he stated.

The Reflection of my Journey to the Republic of South Sudan

"When did you come to South Sudan?" he asked and I told him.

He walked me to the bar and was going to buy me alcohol but I told him I didn't drink and he asked me why I would come to a nightclub and not drink. I said I came here to dance and to enjoy music and he started to laugh and got me an energy drink. We enjoyed our night feeling very happy to meet again after eleven years. He introduced me to all his friends. It seemed like he knew everyone in the club.

By four am I was tired and I called my brother to tell him we are done. Before we left I said goodbye to my childhood friend and his friends. We called my cousins and we left and I was so tired. On our way home we used the same route and the same soldiers recognized our car and they made us go through without checking our car again.

When we reached home we knocked on the door and my sister opened the gate for us. We slept from 5am to around 11am. When I woke up, my father was sitting outside under the tree in the shade, the temperature already racing past 30 degrees. I greeted him and told him it was too hot and brushed my teeth and washed my face.

I grabbed a chair and sat next to him. He started to ask me about my night at the club and I told him it was not good at all. And that it would be the first and last nightclub I attended here in Juba.

He started to laugh very loud and said "It is good, that you have said this. This is why I told you that Juba is not a safe place to walk and you thought that I was refusing to let you go to a nightclub."

A few days later I sat down with my dad and I told him that my main mission that brought me to South Sudan was to join the South Sudan Police Service. He said that was good and asked me about my documents. I told him I had seven recommendation letters from Victoria Police sergeants, inspectors, the Salvation Army and Victoria Police Crime Stoppers and my Year Twelve Education Certificate and I showed them to him.

South Sudan 2015–2017

He said joining the South Sudan Police was very difficult if you didn't have a father, uncle or anyone else who worked in the government or someone in your family who was well known in South Sudan. It's really hard to get in, but I was lucky as my uncle Kuol Manyang Juuk was a Minister of Defence. He was in charge of the entire South Sudan Army. He was a well-respected man in South Sudan.

My father and I went to his house. It was a bit far from our area and around an half an hour drive. Upon reaching his house, we parked outside. My father found his bodyguards sitting outside under the trees in the shade wearing their uniforms with their guns. We asked if he was around.

One of his guards went inside while we and the other guards waited outside. Then his bodyguard came and called us to go inside the house. The house was very nice and big when we got inside. Uncle Kuol got up and greeted me smiling. He was very tall and big, very fit and it was my second time to see him again after eighteen years since 1998 where I first met him in the Narus area in South Sudan. I was very happy to see him again.

He called one of his bodyguards to get us water and soft drinks. I spent more than half an hour talking to him before I told him about wanting to join the South Sudan National Police Service. Our conversations went really well. He started to ask me about my brothers and sisters that I had left behind in Australia and I told him they were good and all doing well except for my older brother. I told him that he was having a lot of issues with the Victoria Police members.

The only hard question to answer that they asked you was the education level that you had completed or the work that you had been doing. You had to explain it to them very well until they understood it. My father, my uncle Kuol Manyang Juuk and the rest of my family all asked me about what I had been doing in Australia for eleven years.

The Reflection of my Journey to the Republic of South Sudan

I replied saying I had been studying and that when I finished Year Twelve I had worked for two years and did some short courses at university. And that I had worked within Victoria Police with the Multicultural Crime Stoppers and Police Service at the watch house. And that I also had been on patrol on the roads with the Salvation Army youth street team.

I explained the work that the Salvation Army does both in and outside the city of Melbourne. My uncle was very happy and wanted to hear more about my experience working with those departments in Australia, especially about my experience with Crime Stoppers in Victoria.

I explained it to him and showed him more pictures of the Victoria Police Crime Stoppers. He confirmed that I had done a lot of great work for my community in Australia. He told me to come back early in the morning around 9am with my dad and copies of my certificates.

I did that early in the morning the next day around seven am. I woke up and had a shower and dressed. I did not even have breakfast and my dad woke up too and we left around eight am for my uncle's house. When we got there we went to meet the General Police Inspector Pieng Deng Majok.

At around nine am we reached his office and I saw a lot of police seated outside his office. All his bodyguards stood up and one with the highiest rank saluted my uncle. My uncle told them to sit. He left me outside for few minutes and went inside Pieng's office.

Soon after, I was called to go inside Pieng's office. I was very excited to meet him for the first time in my life. He started to ask me a lot of questions about my experience with Victoria Police and I took out my certificates and he started to read them. While reading those papers he started to nod his head. He smiled after he finished reading them and said that I had done great work with the Victoria Police and had very good experience. He then started to tell me about the police in South Sudan and training college and how hard it was. I had already begun to worry about training and I told him I would be able to handle it. He wished me good luck with all the training. The interview with him was very good. I thought I would not get through it but I made it.

I was so excited about going to training college. He said that on the 9th of February I needed to report myself to training college. He told me buy sport clothes, shoes and to also report on the 15th of January 2015 at nine am for the graduations of the C.I.D Crimes Intelligence Department at the Rajaf National Police College.

On the day I woke up around 7am and I had a cold shower. After that I dressed up and took my iPad with me. My father came outside and gave me transport money. I took a motorcycle taxi to the college. The driver asked me to pay first, I asked him how much he would charge me to take me there and he said 40 South Sudanese Pounds.

The roads were not that good with too many rocks and dust. When I arrived, I saw a lot of police wearing uniforms carrying their guns walking around everywhere. There were a lot of high-ranking officers. I walked towards one of the officers and told him I had been invited by General Pieng Deng Majok, Inspector General of South Sudan Police. He welcomed me and took me to where I could sit. All the police who were graduating were standing on parade.

It was around thirty degrees and extremely hot. The Police Training College looked very nice surrounded by two big mountains with tall trees and green grass. I asked one of the high-ranking officers there if I could take pictures around here. At first, he refused and I told him I had been invited by General Pieng Deng Majok. He then said OK. I took pictures with my iPad of the police and generals who were there. I saw one of my childhood uncles named Maker Ater. He was standing on parade with his colleagues. I was so happy to see him in uniform and graduating.

I took his picture and congratulated him. They were feeling tired after standing there for so long but this was part of the discipline for uniform wearing public servants in Africa. They stood up for almost seven hours while the temperature raced up to 40 degrees. At around four pm the graduation finished. Everyone began leaving and I told General Pieng I was going home.

I saw one of the police officers sitting in a police car and I asked him if he could drive me to my area. He said yes and was so keen and a very respectful police officer. I got inside his car and we had a very nice conversation along the way. He had been in the police force for four years working as a police officer in South Sudan. When we reached my area, I told him to drop me off at the Jebel Market which is one of the biggest markets in Juba that was close to where I was living. My house was about a ten-minute walk away. He dropped me there and when I got out I thanked him.

I went straight home and saw my father waiting there for me. He was sitting under the tree in the shade having tea. I sat down and he asked me about the graduation. I told him it was fun but the day was so long. I was feeling tired and I took out my iPad and showed him all the pictures I had taken at the graduation ceremony. After that I slept until I woke up at around eight pm. I had dinner and went back to sleep again.

Early in the morning my father woke me up and we went to the South Sudan Migration Centre to get a South Sudan National I. D and birth certificate. These documents were required to join the South Sudan Police training. My father, he is a great man, very social and honest person and a respectful, hardworking man. He likes everything to be done early before the required time.

When we reached the Migration Centre there were a lot of people there already. The line was too long and I told my father to leave me there so he could go to his work. I told him I would be ok to wait in the line. He took out some money, about two hundred South Sudanese pounds for my lunch so I had money in my pocket. I felt bad to take it but I took his money and thanked him and he left me there.

I didn't know anyone to talk to. Everyone looked exhausted. Most seemed very tired from waiting for too long in the line. The staffs were too slow and some were very rude to the customers. Their service was very weak and they were disrespectful to the people. They looked very good in their uniform but were not good at customer service. I was very disappointed to see things not going well in my motherland.

On that day I argued with one of the police officers who worked at the Migration Centre. One of the high-ranking officers came and pulled me aside to talk to me and he told me to calm down. I was very sad and I explained everything to him. He then took my Australian passport and photo. He told me to wait outside and he took them with him into his office. I waited for so long outside and after a few hours later he came back to me and said I could go for lunch now and that when I came back, my documents would be ready.

I left to have lunch, on my own at a restaurant. I met a poor starving child standing on the roadside wearing dirty clothes so I called him and took him to a restaurant to have lunch with me. After our lunch I gave him 50 South Sudanese pounds to keep for his dinner or transport. I came back to the Migration Centre and I waited outside the office.

When the officer saw me he came over with my South Sudan Nationality I. D and birth certificate holding them in his hand. I apologised for arguing with the staff and said that I was just disappointed when watching them being rude to customers and without customers they would not be working in here. I told him I was going to join police training and he was very happy when he heard that.

Then I left and, on my way, home I called my father and I told him that I had my documents and he was happy. He told me to go to his office at the airport. When I arrived, I showed him my documents and then we went for lunch. After our lunch we went and photocopied all my documents and took them to the Police Department's main office.

Chapter 14

My life was full of many unexpected experiences. Some were good, and some were bad. During times of war, mostly bad times occurred more often than good times.

It seems to me that there are reasons why things happen to people. My hope is that after all these years of war in South Sudan someday there will be a joyful moment for me. I do not have many good memories from my past life since the day I left South Sudan to live in the Kakuma refugee camp in north Kenya. Even once I arrived in Australia in June 2005 with my family, I always felt like I was missing something. Of course, indeed, part of me is and was missing as my whole family was not with me in Australia. I never gave up on myself. I always said this horror will end one day and I will enjoy life.

I resisted the pain I was facing. I did not wish for revenge against my foes for what they did to me. I wished for the bad day to get over and hoped for a better tomorrow. I never allowed that weakness to occupy my mind. Instead, I wished to preach the word of peace to my enemies for the sake of freedom in order to save the lives of the innocent. I wished to just speak out only the word of unification. I wanted to make the world aware of the war situation that was going on in my hometown and bring peace among the people and avoid more lives being lost. War is wrong and we are all human beings with only one common goal: the soul. However, the only message you should be saying to your enemies is peace.

The Reflection of my Journey to the Republic of South Sudan

Bear in mind that when you are torturing someone, you are torturing yourself as well. You might not feel it physically but emotionally, maybe not right then, but afterward, in the near future, when peace comes and when justice prevails. My parents used to tell me not to be afraid but to be brave and strong.

Living in constant fear is an absence of love. Living in continual fear is what is actually happening in South Sudan. There they panic and run randomly into the bush. My dream is truly to help people back home by offering the jobs and skills necessary to feed their families and for me to do that I have to provide all resources they will need to see hope and survive and thrive and help others enjoy life as well.

I'm still alive today because I was helped by caring people supported by the UNHCR providing food, medical support and education. I want to give back to my supporters whose feeding me helped me and to do the same thing as well to others who need my help. Peace is often on my mind. I am constantly crying about the future of the orphans in South Sudan.

During my first visit to Juba, the capital city of South Sudan, the traffic panic in Juba displayed the business of war rage.

There were crazy cars and motorcycles on the roads, people were outside walking, shops were open and women and men were selling mangoes and clothes on the roadsides everywhere. There were more holes and bumps on all the major roads. There were also some French bakeries, hotels and apartments on the airport road with very nice rooftop restaurants.

Since the conflict broke out in South Sudan and the country became more insecure with soldiers, police and National Security everywhere. They began to be deployed on all the roads in Juba. I saw them holding AK47 guns walking everywhere. I was scared seeing them carry machine guns.

Life goes on, people do their jobs and try to cope with the

situation the best they can. If I didn't hear it from my family and friends before I went there, I wouldn't have been able to tell that there had been a war in my motherland.

There was fighting, soldiers deserting the army or defecting to the opposition, rebels regrouping, mines, no progress in peace talks, starvation, cholera outbreaks and no way of knowing whether things would improve or get worse.

This was the first time I went to South Sudan. It was in December 2014 and the country was almost at war with the government soldiers and the opposition regime versus the official government. I remember sitting at my gate in Dubai International Airport, waiting to board my flight to Juba, feeling scared and nervous. It felt like standing on a trampoline before diving into deep water. The best advice I got from friends who had visited South Sudan was to keep an open mind and to have no expectations, because there was just no way to be prepared for what I will experience.

With that in mind I decided to relax, stop worrying, observe my surroundings and deal with whatever came my way. At my gate in Dubai I looked around to see what kind of people I was travelling with.

They were mostly men from South Sudan and a few women from South Sudan, most of them older. There were Chinese businessmen, aid workers and people working for the UN. I particularly remember one man from South Sudan. I could recognize the scars on his forehead from pictures I had seen. He was tall and was wearing a brown suit and looked like he could be someone important. However, the reason I remember him is that he had a goatee and was wearing huge, brown round 80's style glasses and on his feet he had fluffy slippers with tiger stripes. I couldn't stop staring and wished I could have taken a picture of him although I knew that the image of him would last in my mind forever.

He looked very funny but he may have been wearing it to feel comfortable. Watching this man and trying to understand who would wear such a fantastic outfit with fluffy tiger slippers, took away most of my fear and nervousness and I only prepared myself to be amazed.

I took one last deep breath and boarded my plane with the sense of having jumped into a deep and unknown ocean.

I was returning to a place that used to be my home, the place we used to hear about from our parents and elders, the country that I belonged to, the country that I used to hear about and where people prayed for peace to come in our church back when I used to live in the refugee camp, where my childhood friends and families lived, yet I feel like I was diving into the unknown.

The war has changed South Sudan and it has changed a lot of people. Once again, I needed to keep an open mind to what I would see and experience. Once again, I needed to take one last deep breath, jump and remember to swim for the surface.

Chapter 15

On the 21st of December I woke up early in the morning feeling strangely rested on a Thursday morning and I heard something like the sound of AK47s firing. It was the neighbour's new, massive and noisy generator.

On the 27th of December, I asked my father if he could give us his car so I could go to my hometown Bor in Jongelei. He did and gave it to my older brother Thon to drive us there. We left Juba around 9am, on our way to Bor Town. I was very excited about going to my village for the first time in my life. On our way to my hometown Bor we saw a woman with her three children and an old man standing on the left hand side of the road waiting for a vehicle that was traveling to Bor so that they could travel with it.

I told my brother to stop as our car had empty seats and I got out and told them to get inside the car. They packed their bags and got inside. We took off and they were happy to get a ride. We exchanged names. They took out money and they gave it to us but my brother refused to take money from them. They thought the car was for business and we told them we were just helping them as our car had empty seats and they thanked us.

We continued our journey. It was crazy inside our car as we were all having a good time. The journey was three hours from Juba to Bor Town. The roads were not very good with too many holes and dust. My brother had to drive slowly on the road until we reached my village. On the way to my village the roadside was

The Reflection of my Journey to the Republic of South Sudan

littered with lots of dangerous old army tanks. Most were burnt or destroyed during the war in South Sudan and abandoned.

It showed me that there had been a heavy war in our hometown. I told my brother to stop at Khoor Makuach which means "the river of Makuach", one of the famous rivers in South Sudan and it was the river where thousands of people had died during the civil war between Northern and South Sudan. There were thousands of stories that I had heard about this river from our elders who passed through there during war time. I got out of the car and I took a picture of it. There was an army tank there and I took a picture of it and we took off continuing our journey to Bor Town.

I was very happy as it was my first time going to my hometown Bor Town. About one hour later we arrived at a place called Mangala. It was once a famous small town. We parked our car and got off and walked to a small restaurant. The restaurant was nice and clean with a lot of traditional pictures inside and we sat and ordered our traditional food. My brother and I ate our traditional dry fish with bread. It tasted nice and afterwards we had black tea.

Mangala was a small town and was busy with shops all lined up along the main road beside the river. I saw a lot of cattle. People with AK47s were protecting the cattle. I walked towards them and I stood a bit far from them and I started to ask one of the cattle's keepers if I could take a picture of the cattle. Then they spoke to me back in their language that I could not understand. It was a language that I had never heard before. My brother saw me and walked toward me very quickly and asked me what's was going on. I explained it to brother in my language which is the Dinka language. He told me to take out my camera and show it to them.

Then afterwards I took out the camera set it up with the flash on to make them more interested in pictures. I showed them the camera. One of them got up with a stick, holding it on his hands and he moved the AK47 gun to his back and walked towards me. I was about to run away but my brother told me to wait. He was a cool man and he came to check our hands very respectfully. He used his hand as a sign language to communicate with us.

I turned on the camera and showed it to him aimed to where his people were sitting. He saw them on the screen of my camera he started to laugh very loudly and was more interested so I started to take more pictures very quickly and I show them to him. He looked very happy and a few minutes later he went to his house not far from this place. We met and he brought traditional milk with him in plastic containers. I took one and I started to drink. It tasted very nice.

I told him thank you and I shook his hand. We could not understand each other's language. I took out two hundred South Sudanese Pounds and I gave it to him. He started to feel happier and we became friends in just those few minutes. Afterwards we left and walked toward our car and got inside and I put down the mirror and started to wave at them. They started to wave back at us with a smiling face. I saw the little girl jumping up and down with two hands waving at us too. It was a nice time with them. This is the only memory I still have of Magala.

We continued our journey and the road was too annoying with too many holes and cows and goats moving across at any time on the road. All drivers have to be very careful on this road. I saw a lot of sad things during our journey to Bor Town. I saw a lot of people with disabilities, missing legs and arms. There were many with war wounds. Many were soldiers shot and wounded during the war in South Sudan.

After this long journey we reached Bor Town. My brother welcomed me to your hometown and I thanked him. The home looked very nice. People were walking around and all looking very happy. I started to tear up. My brother looked at me and told me

The Reflection of my Journey to the Republic of South Sudan

to take it easy. I was inside the car just looking around feeling very excited to be in my home town for the first time.

We drove to a place where people have tea. It was just a small shop with a lot of people sitting around playing cards and dominos. We parked the car and I got out and knelt down and kissed the ground of my hometown people. Locals turned their faces and looked at me getting up with tears in my eyes. My brother told me to get up and I did and I started to wipe my eyes. I could see almost everyone and their faces were on me.

One of them called to my brother. Thon walked towards them and he asked my brother if I was ok. My brother told them that I was and that I had just come from Australia and that it was the first time I had come to my village. They all understood it then and walked towards me and greeted me happily. A few them said "Welcome to your homeland," and I thanked them.

My brother and I sat down under the tree in the shade and we ordered black tea. My brother Thon is well known in my village. Almost half of the people who live there know him very well especially the youth, and on that day, we had a lot of fun and we were surrounded by a lot of boys from my village. They all wanted to hear a lot of stories about Australia and we sat in one place for almost seven hours just talking and making friends with most of them.

It was getting dark and it was six pm. My brother told me to go home and I got up and said goodnight to all of them. Some of the boys told me to stay on. I told them I was tired and that we would meet again before I went back to Juba. We left and got into our car to go home. When we reached home my cousin saw our car. She came close to our car and as we got out, she gave my brother a hug. She didn't know me as I had never met her before. This was my first time meeting her. Thon introduced me as his younger brother. She was happy and gave me a hug too.

Then she went and brought us two chairs and we sat outside under the tree in the shade. It was too hot and almost 30 degrees outside and I was sweating. My cousin brought us a soft drink and cold water from the local small shop. The shop was a mud hut with a small window where people could buy what they needed.

My brother saw our grandfather Angue Juuk coming holding his stick and walking slowly. He was looking very old. Thon told me he was our grandfather. As he was coming, I turned around and saw him and ran towards him calling his name out loud. I gave him a hug and I mentioned my name.

He was very old but he was very happy for me to hold his arm. I walked him to where we were sitting and I too was very happy to see him again after more than eighteen years apart. We sat down and started to talk. Our conversations were very good and he told me I was a big boy now.

The last time he had seen me was in the Kakuma Refugee Camp in around 2001. When he had left to South Sudan, I hadn't seen him again. I was so excited to meet him again.

Afterwards we had dinner and at around eight pm and I was struggling with fatigue from the long drive. I couldn't stay awake any longer and my body felt very tired. I went and took a shower and I came back and said goodnight to them.

My cousin came and showed us where to sleep. I slept very well only to be annoyed by the sounds of mosquitos and frogs in the night. Apart from that I had a good time in Bor enjoying the traditional food and seeing people wearing traditional clothes everywhere. I met most of my childhood friends in Bor and enjoyed my time with them. I walked around happily. I really enjoyed my time breathing with my hometown air.

The main food I enjoyed most was Asida made from flour and fish. I started to like the lifestyle in Bor more than the Juba life. The lifestyle in Bor was good compared to life in Juba. My brother and I decided that we needed to stay in Bor Town for a whole week.

We had to return back to Juba because I was going to start police training on the 9th of February 2015. So we had to go back to Juba to get ready for training college by the 5th of January. When we left we said goodbye to all our family and friends in Bor Town. I told them that I would come back during holiday time or after I finished my training. Most of them were happy to hear these words before we left. It was sad leaving them behind after we had such a good time with them.

On our way to Juba we had a very nice conversation. We were facing many challenges on the road including too many potholes as well as many army check points and vehicle searches. We arrived back in Juba around seven pm and the journey back gave us a lot of pain after sitting in one place on the road for so long.

Chapter 15

Before we started to do police training all the cadets were sent by the recruitment teams to go and do medical checkups in case of any sicknesses. The checkup was done at a police hospital. It was located at Buluk which was the police headquarters. It was the biggest hospital that served all police members in South Sudan.

During the medical checkup a lot of people were found with a variety of sicknesses often making them unfit to join police training in South Sudan. I was very confident that I would pass the medical checkup and I did. The doctor told me that my results were good and that I was fit to go to training college.

I was so happy I rang up my father to tell him about my result. I also felt bad about those who did not make it into the police college. When I reached home my family and friends were really happy and congratulated me on passing the medical checkup.

A few days later our names were posted on the board outside the front gate of the police college. There were big numbers of people with their names on the board who had passed the medical checkup. This included my name and I was happy to see my name on the list. There were 1,200 cadets' names on the board for the Department of Police training college. Those who had their names on the list had to report on the 9th of February 2015 for the start of training.

On the 9th February 2015 early in the morning around 5am my father came and woke me up. I woke up and packed all my training clothes and sports shoes ready for police training. My father was the one driving and taking me to police training college. It was almost one hour away by car.

At around 6.30am we arrived at the training college's main gate. All the police officers were on duty that day. Some of them were sleeping. Only two were on patrol. Those who were sleeping got up with their guns and they started to ask me some questions. I did not understand because they were using Arabic. My father started to reply to them as he knew the language. He told I was a cadet who had come to training college today for police training.

One of them asked my dad why he had brought me so early in the morning instead of after breakfast. My father told them that he was on his way to work and no one else could bring me later. I was the first of the cadets to arrive at the police college. They said OK and that I could take my bags and blankets with me into the college from the main gate. My father wished me goodbye.

He told me to be strong during the training and to do everything that they told me to do. My father used to be a soldier before and he knew that the police training was not easy and this was why he started to advise me before I started training. At the main gate I looked at him and said "OK bye, dad. I will stay strong during our training." Then he left and waved at me while he drove away and I returned the wave.

Then I entered the college. The police college looked very nice with tall trees and tall grass inside the college. Outside it was surrounded by two large mountain ranges. I just began walking around waiting for other cadets to come. I met some of the officers wearing their uniforms and sitting under the trees waiting for us cadets to arrive. I said hello to them by waving at them and they said hello back. One of them said to me welcome to Police College and I thanked him.

At around 10am more cadets started arriving at the police college carrying their bags. By eleven am the weather was getting hot and up to maybe 30 degrees. One of the officers came and started to talk very loudly so everyone turned around to listen to his words. He told us to pack up our bags and go to the main gate which we all did. The training was starting. When we got outside, we saw all the trainers and officers holding big sticks in their hands and they started to talk very rudely to all cadets. I immediately remembered what my father and uncle told me about the hardship of police training. It clicked in my head immediately after I saw officers and trainers with sticks on their hands. We all went outside the main gate.

One of the high-ranking officers came and told us to listen to him. We all turned around and looked at him ready to hear what he was going to tell us. He said "If you are a man or have strong heart then you will step into this college but if you are not strong you will go back home." I hadn't understood what he said but one of the cadets who spoke both languages, Arabic and Dinka, translated the Arabic words for me into Dinka. We all started to get scared from hearing those words and seeing the officers and trainers holding the sticks so seriously.

Next the trainers made us kneel down and put our bags on top of our heads and then begin walking on our knees. The temperature was too hot. They made us crawl on the ground in that hot weather. We were told not to talk to officers or trainers and to just do what we were told. The torture was too high and they also started to beat us with sticks. I was being beaten up by two trainers hitting me on my back with sticks. All the cadets started to scream very loud. Both girls and boys were doing the same training.

Then they told us to put our bags on top of our heads and run around with them. We had to do it. It was part of our training. We were sweating and our clothes began to be drenched wet with sweat.

The training was becoming harder and harder. We all became very tired and some cadets became very sick. The water tank came and the water was poured on us and then they made us roll in dirty water. The temperature was peaking by this time to around 45 degrees. Our bodies becoming very tired and some of the cadets were deliriously sick. Those who were sick were sent to the police college hospital. All the hospital beds became full of cadets. Most of our feet became swollen because of standing for too long on the hot weather. We were then made to stand for over seven hours without moving. If you turned around or moved your body, you were beaten up more.

We were given no time to rest. Most of our time was spent on the training field with both boys and girls doing the same training. It was one pm on the 9th of January and the training was getting much too hard. We were all reaching exhaustion. All the cadets were becoming sick from the torture by the trainers. The trainers continued to make us roll on the ground and in dirty water till we all looked like pigs in a happy mud swamp. We were being tortured to stand in the weather of more than 40 degrees and many cadets were in the police college hospital. I struggled and tried to be strong and pass through this hardship as my father and uncle told me to be strong in the training centre.

Maybe some of those who went to the hospital were not sick but just retreated to take a break from the heavy training. Some of the cadets were considering giving up and leaving training college including myself.

The officers and trainers had a nickname for me. They called me Kawajah. It meant White Man because I always used English to communicate with them. They didn't understand English either. Some of the cadets called me Australian Man or started using Kawajah Man too. My nickname became quickly known by everyone.

I became well known in our training college by the trainers, officers and cadets. With some infamy I started to make friends with them. I was becoming famous.

South Sudan 2015–2017

In our police training college, we had to attend four parades: the morning parade, the afternoon parade, the evening parade and the night parade.

Every morning around four am we would wake up for morning tea. We had another whistle for morning parade at five thirty am and the officers who were unchanged had to count all cadets who had attended parade.

Those who did not attend morning parade got their names put on separate list and they were tortured for not attending parade. Those who did come had no problem.

After counting us on parade we went for fitness running around the training college or went outside the college and ran on the main road. Over 1,000 cadets ran on the road and we all sang. We sang our police songs very loudly and people who lived in the small village near our police college came out and watched us.

Sometimes we ran carrying an AK47 holding it in our hands. Every time when we returned from running we always felt tired. Then at around ten am we had an early lunch and after we finished eating we had to prepare ourselves for classes. We had two different classes, English patterns and Arabic patterns.

Classes went until 2.30pm. Sometimes we didn't have teachers to come and teach us in our English classroom because most of the teachers who taught us had high ranks and were mostly attending different meetings for police work. So most of the time we sat in the classroom reading law books on our own. The police college was very poor on this front.

During our training I caught malaria and typhoid and my body became very weak and I was throwing up badly. The ambulance came and took me to hospital. My body became very thin. I couldn't walk properly. I found my life very useless And I felt like it was the end of my life.

The Reflection of my Journey to the Republic of South Sudan

The police college administration rang up my father to come and take me to Juba for further treatment. My father came and he saw me lying down on the floor. My body was shaking and feeling cold despite the temperature being 50 degrees.

My father came and woke me up by calling my name loudly. I looked up and saw him. I gave him my right hand and he pulled me up as I did not have the power to stand up myself. I felt powerless in my body. I got in his car and he took me to hospital. It was one of the expensive local pharmacies for better treatment. I got about five injections in my body for malaria because the malaria infection level was too high.

My body lost a lot of weight. I looked like a skeleton. My entire family began to worry a lot about me. My sister shed tears when she saw me. I couldn't feel my body at all.

South Sudan's weather wasn't really good and it messed me up a lot. I laid down on the bed and going to the toilet was very difficult. Every time I ate or drank any juice I vomited. The doctors and my family tried their best to make me feel better.

One day I woke up in the middle of the night with an empty stomach feeling like I wanted to eat. My dad was sitting next to me and it was nighttime. He was still awake and worried about me. Then he asked me how I was feeling.

I told him I wanted to eat and that I was really starving now. He went and got me juice and fruits. Early in the morning my sister came with more food and fruits. My body was very tired. The malaria and typhoid had become worse. A few hours later the results came. The doctor told my dad the cause of this malaria was from drinking dirty water and weather conditions, because in the training college they drank River Nile water. They didn't have a clean water tap. The police college had more than ten large containers and we drank from those. We also showered with that water because we had no other option.

South Sudan 2015–2017

After I was released from hospital my father decided to buy me a twenty litre jerry can of clean water. I took it to the police college every week and brought it home to refill every Sunday afternoon. I would return to Police College with it every weekend. It became a big job for me and I had to do it to reduce the chance of sickness. I became well after I started to drink clean water from the company. I stopped drinking dirty water from River Nile. I also give my colleagues some clean water by sharing it with them. Afterward my body become normal I started to do training with my colleagues back to hardship again similar to the first day when we first entered the Rajaf National Police College on the 9th of February 2015.

When we got to crawl and roll on the ground the rocks in the soil hurt us a lot. Our bodies had many bruises, especially our knees and arms that became very painful. Life had become hard. The weather was too hot usually 40 degrees or more. We had to stand in the hot weather for more than six hours a day. It tortured us too much and a lot of the sick cadets could not help themselves the way I had done. Our life in the Rajaf National Police College was a seemingly useless life.

I blamed myself for being there but it was a great experience to be there at the same time. We also ran every morning for fitness.

On the 15th of February, one week later, one of our colleagues named David was sick during our training because of the heavy training we were doing. I was standing on parade and one of the officers pointed his finger at me and a female colleague in our platoon. He said get out with a rude voice so we rushed out quickly. I was panicking.

We saw David our colleague. His body was shaking on the ground and he was crying loudly too. The officer called an ambulance and when it arrived, we picked up David's body from the ground and put him into the ambulance. I got in the ambulance as well. When we reached the police college hospital, we got David off but couldn't walk him properly. I held his arm assisting him to the hospital room.

All night I was just sitting near David, worried about him. In the middle of the night his sickness was getting worse and it seemed like he couldn't breathe. He stopped breathing completely. Early in the morning around six am I went to doctor's office with tears in my eyes. I told him David was not breathing. The doctor came and checked him then he started to nod his head. From there I knew it was bad.

A few minutes later he told me that David had passed away. The death of my colleague David made my body collapse with sadness. I was just sitting there on the chair near his body feeling sad and crying. It was first time in my life experiencing this kind of situation.

One hour later one of the doctors went to the police administration office. It was eight am and he reported the death to the police college principal and high-ranking officers. One of the officers came to the hospital and found me sitting there and crying. We sat there for few hours waiting for the death certificate from the doctor so we could take David's dead body to his family. They called his family so we could meet them at the Juba Teaching Hospital to receive his body. After we got the letter from doctor, we put David's body into ambulance and left. It took us almost one hour to reach the Juba military hospital and when we arrived, we found a large number of David's family waiting for us.

We found them crying and screaming very loudly in grief. The doctor and I and one of the officers opened the back door of the ambulance. David's family members came near the car crying and waiting to see his body. We told them to wait for a bit for us to bring his body out from the car for everyone to see his body. I myself started to cry. It hurt me a lot to lose my colleague so easily like this.

Later on, we took David's dead body out from the ambulance. His family started to cry more when they saw his body and it was getting worse and out of control. We took his body inside the mortuary where they kept the dead bodies. I was the one who took his body inside. I saw two other dead bodies inside there that made me go crazy. I had never experienced this in my life before. I was seeing multiple dead bodies.

Afterwards we left David's body with his family and we came back to police training college. When we arrived, I found all my colleagues standing on parade all feeling sad about David's death. The officer who was in charge that day told me to go and take a rest in our room. When I slept, I couldn't stop thinking about David and seeing those dead bodies. I sat down with tears in my eyes. I started to pray silently to God asking him to keep David in a safe place and to bless his family too. He was our hero. We could not forget him.

David was the only child of his mum and dad and he didn't have any brothers or sisters. His parents had already passed away. He was being brought up by his close relatives. One week later after the death of David, I started to do activities. I kept myself busy to stop myself from thinking too much about David and the other dead bodies that I saw in the hospital. I became better after a few weeks and got back to a normal life. I still remember him today and still respect him as my colleague.

It is strange the things we do in South Sudan in the name of "It's Our Culture". We care more for the dead than we do for the living. We spend more time to bury a person than we do to save their life when they are sick. We will not see a sick relative when they are in hospital but we will travel to bury him or her when they die. People will rarely respect you while alive but will want to pay their last respects, to your casket crying when they see you dead and your body lying on the ground. A person may never receive roses in their entire life but they will get lots dumped on their grave. We will spend a night at a neighbor's funeral and it will be our first time to see the inside of their house.

No one gives a damn to know your village until you die and then they will fill car after car to escort your corpse to the same village. We will take the dead to the mosque or temple or church knowing full well that they had nothing to do with worship or religion while alive. We might not have granite tops in our kitchens but we use the granite in the graveyard. An entire village might not have a single house with cement floors but the only place with cement will be a graveyard. We say how dear a person was to us after he died. When he is alive, we do not tell them. I propose that we have cultural reforms. We have a culture of hypocrisy. A culture that is pro-death and not pro-life. We need to value life before death.

Please love me while I am alive today. Show me that you care about me. Show me your kindness that I need now, as your presence at my funeral, friends, or your family members will never make up for your absence when I have the greatest need of you. Do it now for me to enjoy.

The above got me thinking.
I met you as an unknown one,
Now I have you as a friend.
I hope we meet in our next walk of life where friendship never ends.

I may not be the most important person in your life. I just hope that when you hear my name, you smile and you say "That's my friend."

Let's change this culture and love the way God loves us. Let's put our hands together and save the lives of sick vulnerable people not only in South Sudan but all around the world.

In our police college, every morning after our breakfast we went to our law classrooms. We had two different classrooms, Arabic and English. Arabic was the first language in our police college followed by English. The majority of cadets including our trainers and officers spoke Arabic. I found it very hard to communicate with a lot of my colleagues and trainers because of my lack of knowledge of Arabic. During our training I suffered a lot because the trainers spoke Arabic.

I felt like I was in a different world. A lot of my colleagues wished to talk to me and ask me about life in Australia but couldn't because they didn't know English. They found it very hard to communicate with me as I only communicated with those who spoke English or Dinka. Our training continued and things were still getting harder. The weather conditions were still around 45 degrees.

During the training some of my colleagues who could speak and write English were selected to be sent to Uganda and Rwanda for further police training. My name was on the list of people who were going to Uganda but I was not willing to go. I told the officers to replace me with someone else. I was happy to stay back so I could go to Juba every weekend and see my family. I really wanted to spend as much time with my family as I could. In our police college I had become increasingly friendly with all my colleagues and officers. I found it very difficult to leave them behind again by going to Uganda. I was happy to stay back with them. My position was given to another cadet who was willing to go to Uganda.

I became well known in Rajaf Police College and well respected as well by all my colleagues and trainers. At our police training college, training was very hard and the level of teaching was very low. We didn't have enough teachers who could teach in English. We had only three teachers and they didn't come most of the time so we stayed in our classroom without teachers. Sometimes we

The Reflection of my Journey to the Republic of South Sudan

would go for a week or more on our own. We just read all the law books on our own. We had to put more energy into studying and reading all the law books. Some cadets found it difficult to read the books without a teacher.

The reason teachers didn't come to teach us was because most of them were high ranking officers and worked in the police headquarters. They were always busy there and transport was very difficult. Most of them used their own pocket money to put fuel in their vehicles and the college was too far from where most of them lived. We just sat our bums on the chairs in our classroom and read law books. We stayed in classroom until two pm and then went for afternoon parade.

Our training and classes continued from 9th February 2015 until 8th March 2016. By this time all the cadets dreamt about graduating from police training college. We all became tired of staying in training college eating food that included rice and beans. We just wanted to get out quickly and work. But we still had a long way to go. Life wasn't easy in the police college.

At the college we lacked a lot of things. Sometimes we had no water and the hospitals mostly ran out of medicines. The doctors from the police college hospital gave transfer medical papers to Juba hospital so cadets could get better treatment. When they returned to the training college, they had to show a letter from the hospital they got treatment at to the college administration so they could witness that this cadet had been in Juba hospital and had treatment there.

If a cadet who was sick was still not feeling well they were told to stay in their rooms and not to attend activities. They allowed them to attend morning parades, afternoon parades, and night parades but not to do any activities until they got better.

I found South Sudan life totally different to Australian life. South Sudan is a new born country. It just ended a war in 2005. Then the peace agreement was signed between North Sudan and South Sudan ending 22 years of civil war. This made the life of people who had grown up or were born in western countries hard when they returned to a new country like South Sudan. Police, National Security, and Army were all very poor and without much equipment and resources. The majority of the persons in these jobs were uneducated and they had little if any background in education. This was one of the challenges the people of South Sudan were facing.

For them to deal with surveillance for example, people in public areas always turned to violence. Police and other forces mistreated surveillance badly in public areas.

Rajaf National Police College was very big with tall trees and green grass. It is surrounded by two large mountains. Snakes, scorpions and lizards run around every night and even during the day. Two of my colleagues were bitten by snakes and luckily, they are still alive.

The names of my colleagues that I used to share a room with:

1. Angelo Ayieny Aduot
2. Michael Mayen Arol
3. Panyido Majak Barkuei
4. Akeen Garang Akeen
5. Luka Mohammed Mungu
6. Deng Bol Age I
7. Hafis sabet
8. Akol Akola Deng
9. Adil sebit Jalal
9. Auothodu sebit
10. Kuot Manyang
11. Marin Akuin
12. Garang Mabior

The Reflection of my Journey to the Republic of South Sudan

The names of my colleagues that used to be in my platoon:

Abraham Ajang,
Athiu Mabior
Atak Tito
Emmanuel Lado
Jodes Michael
Nielson Georage
Pijo John
Daniel John
Sabino James
Agada Solomon
Leek Garang Leek
Dheui Majok
Kuol Deng Kuol
Majur John
Chan Makir
Joseph john
William Gule
Deng Bul
Ariel Majak
Tito Abol
Giet Alak
Malap Andrea

Chapter 16

While I was in the police training college I started to help South Sudan street children and people with disabilities. It started when one day when I was going to Juba Town to receive money that was being sent to me by one of my friends in Australia.

On my way there I saw a child lying down in the doorway of a shop. I walked past her to the bank. When I reached the bank I had to wait for almost half an hour because a lot of people were there waiting to receive their money too.

After I received my money I left to go back the same way. I saw this same young girl again on the same spot lying down. I walked towards her and woke her up. She got up and seemed starved. I asked her if she wanted to eat and she said "Yes."

I took her to a restaurant within Juba Town and I ordered food and drink for her. I waited until she finished eating and then I paid for her food. Before I said goodbye to her, I asked for her name and she told me its Margaret and that her family were alive but that they were poor. This was what made her to go on the street to look for food.

She thanked me with tears in her eyes and I told her it was ok and she stopped crying. I took out one hundred South Sudanese Pounds (Equivalent $7 or $8 AU) and I gave it to her for her dinner.

Then I left for home and on my way home I saw a lot of children just walking around everywhere in the market. I realised that they were street children. They were poor kids, some with families that could not provide for them. I teared up because of seeing these children suffering on the streets and no one helping them.

I went back to our Police College. One day I went to the Nile River in South Sudan and I sat down under a tree in the shade. I could see the water flooding on the river and as I was looking around, I remembered the street children and thought a lot about them.

I said to myself that I wished I was a rich person so I could help all of them out. I would send most of them to school to have better education and a better life but because I was poor, I didn't have anything and I would just leave it to God.

Luckily, I had a lot of friends and they used to send me money every month. Sometimes one hundred U.S.D. or more. I didn't do much with the money while I was living in South Sudan because I spent most of my time at the police training college. I only went to Juba for a weekend and came back on Sunday afternoon or evening.

I started to help some of the street children by buying them food, clothes and thongs. While doing that job I faced several challenges. There were a lot of street children all with the same conditions and all needing help. Each time I ran out of money so I promised some that the next weekend or next time I saw them that I would help. It became harder and harder.

I began to build up a lot of stress. I wanted to help all these kids but the money was not enough. I couldn't help all of them. I began to take their photos and upload the street children photos on my Facebook and write about their life stories and share it on my Facebook timeline. A lot of people saw it and they encouraged me to do more to continue helping these innocent children. Most of them lived in western countries and they started to send me money through Amal Express and Dahabshill Banks to help my program.

South Sudan 2015–2017

I found a lot of children very sick with malaria and their feet were often swollen with a lot of bruises there and on other parts of their bodies. I took some of them to the local clinic and got some treatment for them with my pocket money. I became well known by most of these street children. I became like a father figure to them.

I saw them as future leaders. Every time I passed near them, they always called me with my name or they called me uncle. Some got up and walked towards me and shook my hand in a respectful way. I felt happy to help the poor children.

I never forgot that I was helped by the United Nations (UN) high commissioner of refugees for thirteen years of my life whilst living in the Kakuma Refugee camp in Kenya. At the camp they provided us with clean water, food, medicine and education. Without this many of us would have died. I look back and have an urge to help poor people in the way I used to get help from others.

It is only in recent years in Juba the capital of South Sudan that there has been a problem of street children. It is a problem attributed to the long civil war in the Sudan.

Briefly before I moved to South Sudan to stay there for two and half years, I started to do a lot of research regarding children living on the street in South Sudan. I initially found one article for this topic, a little bit dated, titled "The power of street children in this country". It interested me quite a lot and so I started searching for more recent and related areas around main markets of South Sudan Juba business centres.

Unfortunately, these were not easy to find and my Internet perusing began to lose its focus since much detail was often ignored by the few of readers and there were missing website links. As I looked through the most recent reports of child suffering, I found an incredibly moving speech about the unjust street children system in the South Sudan. Through their words I began to recognize

The Reflection of my Journey to the Republic of South Sudan

meaningful connections between their ideas and became a friend to them.

From there I wrote about their problems. What is a street child? Some of the readers may ask this question: "Who is street child?". Street children are minors who live and survive on the streets daily. They often grow up in public landfills, bus stations and under the bridges of the world's major cities. Because of conflicts with their family, these children do not want to or cannot return home forcing them to live on the streets here in South Sudan or around the world.

In South Sudan today, most of the children may be forced to the streets due to a number of reasons around the globe, some of which are mentioned here:

- Overcrowding: (A lack of living space, poor house ventilation, etc. under which children are forced to live in slum areas without food and other basic amenities has forced numerous children to the streets of cities.

- Negative attitudes toward children such as the abusive work in homes where domestic workers are forced to run away as a result of being overworked underpaid or even subjected to other forms of abuse. They end up on the streets trying to earn a living.
- The growing HIV/AIDS scourge in Africa has left many children orphaned or abandoned by their parents. Such children often end up as street children. With one third of Africans now living in towns and cities, coupled with rapid urban population growth rates, the streets have become the workplace and playground for millions of street children where their lives are at risk.
- Generally the poverty level in urban areas is on the increase and children have no choice but to go out and look for their

daily bread to assist their younger siblings. In the case of single female headed households a child may feel the need to go out and assist his/her mother in bringing some income.
- Family crisis: poverty and other associated life events may result in dysfunctional parenting styles. These weaken family bonds and result in an environment where parents become physically and emotionally abusive to their children or towards each other.

Some children have got many jobs to do like selling empty containers, collecting garbage, selling juice, green mango or lemons, polishing shoes etc. to help them survive.

When I asked some of the street children where they got food both lunch and supper, they told me that they had got nowhere to get food, shelter or housing for lodging. They sleep at the corners of buildings in the markets using cotton and they used their already worn clothes for covering themselves if it became cold. The international NGOs operating in South Sudan focus only on government affairs forgetting what they should be doing to help the kids living on the streets of the country. Our beloved children who are sometimes called the foundation of nationhood are deserting their homes due to uncontrollable reasons.

Kids living on the cold streets of South Sudan are the dangerous enemies to the country's insecurity and crimes because there are so many "pull" factors that can help make the street attractive to a child. These play a role in leading some children into street situations. A lack of family nurturing and support, mistreatment from stepparents, a lack of family norms/regulations, a lack of education, the death or divorcing of parents, all play a key role.

Street kids do the following: they play wall kid, scripts, play games, play football in the street, play basketball in the street, they steal people's handbags in the streets, they embarrass buyers in the markets, they present a bad image to the non-citizens of South Sudan, they beg at the road side, and they caused a traffic jam when crossing the streets. When I researched the main markets of Juba, I found out that women who always shop in the markets are the most victimized.

Kids who live on the streets of the markets steal women's small handbags and run away with them. No one was around that could run after those children. The only means for the women is just shake their head and cry loudly thinking that the loud voice will help bring her bag back. The question that anybody with a sound mind should ask is, where do you think these children will end up from practicing such behavior's?

Also, the women need to carry their handbags in their hands, not like men who keep their small coins in the pocket where it takes time for a thief to put his/her hands inside.

South Sudan street children are our children: they are humans and we are humans.

They breathe. They smile or cry. They listen and talk. They move, jump, sit and stand. They need food, water, shelter and clothes. They dream, wish and hope they live and grow into a very important person, one day. They want to learn, become doctors, lawyers, engineers or business people. Let's get them off those streets because they want to succeed, just like us. They are part of our community and everyday life. These children are innocent kids. They are South Sudanese. We need to work hard and help the people of South Sudan. They are in our streets. They are in our markets everywhere. They shine our shoes, clean our cars, eat our leftovers in guesthouses or restaurants. They are everywhere around us.

Whether as a community or a society, they are part of our community. They need our help from community-based organizations or civil society organizations.

They have brains and they can think. They decided to leave home and find "paradise" on the streets. If we help them, they can decide to abandon street life and go back home if they can rather than living on the streets. They can go back to school. They can learn and become good citizens of South Sudan.

They have the potential to become good adult men and women. They are growing up now. They will become strong men and beautiful women. They have the potential to become good citizens or bad people. If we get them off the streets, they can go to school, learn and become doctors, lawyers, engineers, business people, police or pilots. One day, they can be leaders or members who will build our nation or help other street children or other poor people in the future. And if we don't help them now, they can grow into criminals who can destroy our lives and properties in South Sudan.

They just didn't know what living on the streets would look like in the future. In the first place, it was not their fault to stay hungry at home. It wasn't their fault if their parents died and left them an orphan. It's not their mistake that a parent is an alcoholic or can't provide food. It wasn't their mistake to leave home to look for food elsewhere. Let's not ignore them or punish them by denying them our help. We can help them in one way or another. Let's help them because they cannot help themselves. They do not know we can help them but we know we can! Street children are our children!

These are my goals:

Main Objective:

My South Sudan Street Children Leaders Of Tomorrow program aims to address the protection of street children's rights, both boys and girls, in line with national, regional and international norms. The program aims to develop projects which support the development of children and create a peaceful community co-existence where issues of conflicts are settled amicably for justice to take its course.

Specific Objectives South Sudan Street Children will address the two key principles of child rights

1. The right to survival and development;
2. The right of all children to enjoy all the rights of the Convention without discrimination of any kind.

75 % of street children of Juba have explicitly expressed their desire to go back to school and finish their primary education. Therefore, supporting their education development both formally and informally is the Oxfam IBIS' priority and is built upon our expertise in the education sector in South Sudan.

Shelter

The majority of street living children do not have permanent sleeping places during the night. They keep moving from one place to another, in search of a safe corner where the possibility of being raped, robbed or harassed is minimized. This is especially a priority for the girls who are in danger of becoming victims of sexual violence first and of sexual exploitation later.

Economic and family re-integration

Most of the parents of street children lack employment because they are de-mobilised soldiers not yet integrated back into the society and are mainly returnees from Khartoum and not familiar with Juba or village dwellers unskilled or unable to find a job in the city. The implementation of income-generating activities contributes to their economic reintegration into the society while facilitating the re-integration of their children from the streets to their families.

Capacity building and awareness

Police and security officers perceive street children negatively and treat them abusively. A set of standard operating procedures that ensures the child's right to protection are developed for police and government stakeholders who, through trainings and skills development, can improve their relationships with children in street situations and influence the community positively. Counterparts at the Ministry of Social Development and organisations are already working with street children to form the core team in project coordination and will require professional skills and knowledge.

The girls are usually less visible than boys, probably because they work as domestic workers during the day. However, the lack of shelter at night has made them particularly at risk of sexual violence, which has proved to be the first step for girls into the sex industry.

Most of the parents of children in street situations are former soldiers who are not yet integrated in the current society. The parents are generally unemployed.

The children who live on the immediate outskirts of Juba, in semi-rural shanty towns, have a generally positive social network, probably due to the fact that they are still in contact with their families and return home at night. But this is not the case for those children who live in the city centre, around Juba's main markets and trading areas. They are perceived by the public as outcasts and are often treated in a hostile manner. If they spend the night outdoors they are continually harassed by the local police and often imprisoned.

Shelter is especially a priority for the girls who are in danger of becoming victims of sexual violence first and of sexual exploitation later.

With one of the highest infant mortality rates in the world, a chronically malnourished population and recurring epidemics, South Sudan faces a considerable challenge when regarding access to healthcare. In effect, according to Doctors Without Borders (MSF), 75% of the population does not have access to basic healthcare and 80% of healthcare services are provided by international NGOs. There are only 120 doctors and a hundred or so nurses to cater for eight million South Sudanese citizens.

The healthcare situation is critical, particularly for children. A girl of fifteen years is more likely to die during childbirth than go to school. In addition, more than 80% of South Sudanese have no access to toilets.

The government faces an immense task in dealing with the lack of qualified staff and healthcare facilities in order to meet the needs of its people. Added to this issue is an additional pressure on the healthcare system due to the return since independence of 300,000 South Sudanese from the North and the continued instability of the country.

With 550,000 HIV positive persons in South Sudan, children find themselves powerless against the spread of the virus. A population particularly affected by this epidemic are the street children. In effect, they receive almost no family support, no education and still much less protection, and find themselves more and more often confronted with grave dangers such as sexual abuse and HIV to which they are particularly vulnerable since they are unaware of its mode of transmission.

Furthermore, the increased interactions with neighbouring Uganda and Kenya, which are largely affected by the HIV epidemic increase the risk of contamination of South Sudanese children. The government still has much more to do in the fight against AIDS.

No one knows the exact number of street children that South Sudan, and its capital Juba in particular, harbours. These children, who sleep on the streets, are one of the consequences of the 21 years of civil war that has ravaged the region. The majority of them do not even remember their families from whom they were torn when they had to flee their villages in the grip of violence.

While I was in South Sudan, I was living in this area named Khoor Willang. It is one of the famous areas in Juba and is near the Army Baracks. It is surrounded by a lot of shops and is a very nice place. The majority of people who live there are soldiers but only a few survive there today. It's a busy place with loud music in the market place and shops open from eight am to ten pm. That's when the electricity generators go on in a market and they also make a lot of noise.

I used to go there when I left the police training college for the weekend. I met a lot of people around there and became close friends to a lot of people who I am still in contact with now.

One day I was at that market having tea with my friends and two of my cousins Chol Kulang and Arou Aborish Arou turned up. While having tea one of the disabled kids came crawling along on the ground wearing dirty clothes. The kid was just an innocent child. He passed near us and when I saw him, I called and I put my hand in my pocket and pulled out two hundred South Sudanese Pounds and I gave it to him. He thanked me.

I told him to stay with us and have tea as well and he did. Almost all the people who are in that market know him very well. He jokes around with people and he is very friendly with the people there. After we had tea, he left crawling back to his house. He lives not far from the shopping centre and his name is Ladoli Wani. He is a disabled man.

After the weekend I went back to our police training college. I was only there one day and night and I was sleeping at our police college when in the middle of night, I had a dream about this young boy Ladoli. I saw his picture through a dream where he was crawling on the ground and talking to me. I woke up after half an hour. I went back to sleep. While sleeping again I had another dream about him. When I woke up this time it was three am and I couldn't go back to sleep again until five am.

We got up and went for morning breakfast and after breakfast we prepared for morning parade and fitness. We came back from morning fitness and I shared the dream with my colleagues. They told me it was God who sent that dream to me and I needed to meet with this boy and his family. It was Wednesday morning and on the same day I received a phone call from one of my friends who is now in Australia. He told that he had sent me 300 USD to the Dahabshill bank.

I walked to the main office and asked for permission to go to Juba and receive money from the bank. I was given permission and the officer who was on duty that day told me to stay in Juba until the weekend and return back on Sunday afternoon to the college. I took the permission letter and I told my platoon team leader that I was going to Juba so he could be aware of it and let the other officers know as well.

I left for Juba and on my way there I was thinking about this dream and I was worried. When I reached the bank I walked to the counter and I gave my ID and the name of the person who sent me money. They gave me the money and I exchanged it to South Sudanese pounds so I received twenty thousand South Sudanese pounds.

I went home. When I reached home I called my sister and I shared with her the dream I had had at the police college about a disabled kid named Ladoli. She told me to go and meet with him. I walked outside and I went to a market where I saw him the first time I had met him and I asked people around there and found another one of the boys I knew.

He told me that he would take me to his house. So we walked there and when we reached his house and I saw Ladoli Wani and his mother seating under the tree in the shade. They got up to greet us. She went and got chairs for myself and the young boy who had taken me to his house. The boy said he wanted to go back to the market and left. I remained with Ladoli and his mother.

I could not understand their language as they spoke in Arabic of which I only knew a few words. She went and called a guy who spoke both languages, Arabic and English, to do some interpreting. When I saw Ladoli I cried a lot feeling sad seeing the poor child Ladoli with his mother. She told me not to cry and I started to explain the dream I had had. While talking I was crying as well. Ladoli's mother told me God had made Ladoli disabled. It was God who had created him to be like this.

I took out 5000 South Sudanese pounds and I gave it to her. She was very happy with Ladoli when I gave them money. Ladoli's father Mr Abudijo Jada Wani was killed by the Northern Sudan president in Khartoum in 1997 during the war between North Sudan and South Sudan. He was part of the South Sudan government.

Before I left I asked Ladoli what I could help him with and he told me that he only needed a wheelchair. I took his photo with his mother and I uploaded them on Facebook with his life story and a lot of my friends on Facebook saw it and they began to call me on messenger. They sent me a lot of messages regarding Ladoli Wani all feeling sad about him and they started to send me money from America and Australia to give it to Ladoli and his mother.

One of the South Sudanese girls named Adut Akechak who lived in Melbourne was the first person who call me and sent 150 USD to me to give it to Ladoli Wani family. Ladoli became a close friend to me and my best friend. I took him as part of my family as well. Afterwards I bought him a secondhand wheelchair from the market for four thousand South Sudanese Pounds and took it to his house.

The Reflection of my Journey to the Republic of South Sudan

When Ladoli's mother Mrs Marsalina Keji Loro saw me coming with a wheelchair she was happy and started to cry. I saw Ladoli smiling feeling happy as well. Ladoli Wani thanked me. I am still helping Ladoli Wani.

In the year 2016 I went to Jebel Market, one of the largest markets in South Sudan. It was a busy market and I wasshopping. I saw a street child named Abu Sallah. I walked towards him and I called him to come and have lunch with me. He was the second child I helped in South Sudan.

Abu Sallah lived with his poor mother. His dad had passed away is what he told me after I asked him about his family while having lunch. Abu spent most of his time on streets of South Sudan looking for food to survive his daily job. He was a shoe polisher and took whatever money he made to his poor mother. It made me feel sad seeing a child like Abu suffering on the street.

He could have been at school studying but because of the poverty of his family he stayed on the street polishing shoes to survive. After I had lunch and a nice conversation with Abu, I took him to a shop and bought him new clothes and shoes. Abu became my good friend after I helped him and we started to catch up every weekend.

One day he told me to go to his house and meet with his poor mother Teresa which I did and I was very happy to do so. I walked to his house not far from Jebel market. At his house I met his mother. They live in a small mud hut house with his mother and two of his brothers. I sat down and I talked to his mother. I had some money and I took out 500 South Sudanese pounds and I gave it to his mother. She was happy and thanked me.

Before I left his house, Abu asked me if I could buy him a school bag and other material's as he was willing to go to school and have a better education. I told him I would help him. A week later I bought Abu's school materials and I took him to the Guida primary school not far from where he lives. It's right next to an army barrack. When we arrived at the school, we walked to the school principal's office and I told the principal to register Abu. I had to pay 1000 South Sudanese pounds for the school registration and Abu was then a student at Guida Primary School. I was happy to see Abu going to primary school rather than staying on the streets of South Sudan.

I had a lot of challenges seeing a lot of kids on the streets and the government doesn't help them. I wish I had the power to send a lot of kids to school. But because of a lack of funds I could not always do it.

Sometimes I sit down and I think too much about street kids. Sometimes I cry in my heart and tears come out in my eyes. I don't even worry about myself that much. I worry a lot about poor people in South Sudan. This was one of the greatest challenges I was facing in my motherland South Sudan. Street children are being mistreated by the government, especially by police officers beating them up and chasing them on the street like animals. I see them as our future leaders. I was really keen to help these kids out. Most of them are sick and they never meet with doctors because they don't have money to pay for their treatments in hospital.

I go to Guida primary school sometimes to visit Abu Sallah to see he is doing well. He participates a lot in class and he is really into school. All the teachers are happy with Abu. He always goes on time in school and he never takes a day off. I am so happy to see him participate in school. He studies hard, he told me and he wants to be a doctor in South Sudan and help people out in the future. Abu never went back to the street since he began to go to school.

One thing that disturbs him a lot is when he goes to school with an empty stomach. It makes him very weak at school and this is one of the big challenges children also face in South Sudan.

But they are willing to study and become better people in South Sudan. The majority of them die on the streets before they reached eighteen years of age. The government of South Sudan never see these children as humans. If they did, they could help the children rather than letting them struggle on the streets. I never gave up. I continued helping the street kids and every time I got money I helped as much as I could to save their life.

If I died and go to heaven or wherever people go to when they die, I will have people who will remember me all their lives. Street children and people with disabilities that I used to help in South Sudan, they will never forget me and they will remember me forever.

Chapter 17

When I was helping street children and those with disabilities the college principal of police found out and disliked it. He arrested me and sentenced me to imprisonment in the Juba Central prison in the year 2016.

On Monday the 23rd of June 2016 I wrote on Facebook the words that I remember very well. This is what I wrote on Facebook: The Generals of South Sudan are very happy that their children are happy. Most of them have their children outside of the country and they live in Uganda and Kenya happily. While the rest of children who don't have fathers or uncles working in South Sudan are the ones suffering in South Sudan.

This was careless and I posted it on Facebook while I was inside the Police College. A lot of people commented on it. Some said that these words were true and they agreed with my words on the 24th of June 2016.

I was very sick with malaria. I couldn't feel my body in a temperature of 40 degrees. I was feeling very cold. Early in the morning I was in the police college as we normally had morning parade and our alarm as whistle from the officers or cadets who were in charge. They blew a whistle around five am to wake us up every morning. I couldn't get up from my bed.

The same night I had a bad dream. In my dream there was a snake chasing a mouse and a black cat chasing both of them. In my dream seeing all of this, I started to scream very loud and most of my colleagues who shared a room with me all woke up. My colleague Mayen Arol whose bed was next to my bed woke up and he started to call my name. After three times I responded back and he asked if I was ok. I remain silent and my body began to shake. My colleague Mayen went and got me water. He told me to drink the water and I did and thanked him and went back to sleep.

Around five thirty am was the time we normally went for morning tea before we went to the training centre. Mayen Arol also went to get me a tea as he was so worried about me. I sat down on my bed thinking about this dream. It was the worst dream I had ever had. I had never had a bad dream before.

All my colleagues went to the training centre and I remained inside our room. My platoon team leader reported to the officers on duty that I was sick and couldn't attend morning parade. My sickness was getting worse and worse.

When the cadets returned from morning parade Mayen Arol and my colleague Pinydo Majak Barkuei walked towards my bed and saw me laying down with tears in my eyes. Pinydo went to the administration office and reported it to the officer who was in charge that day. The officer told him to come and take me to the office. When he came back he told me to get up on my bed. I couldn't walk properly so Pinydo held my arm and walked me to the office. When we reached the office, I was given a permission letter to go to Juba for further treatment because our police college hospital had run out of medicine.

Pinydo my colleague came with me. It was morning after we got that letter from the officer and we walked back to our room. I went and packed my clothes and I told Pinydo to sleep for a bit before we went. I slept until three pm and when I woke up we left for the hospital. We went to the Juba military hospital, one of the largest hospitals in South Sudan. When we reached the Juba military hospital Pinydo took me to the doctors and explained to them about my sickness.

One of doctors came and took me to the room for a checkup. They found that the level of malaria was very high in my body so I was given injections three times. The doctor gave me malaria tablets and I sat down for a bit before we left the hospital. I took a good rest and at around six thirty pm we left the hospital to go home. I live not far from the hospital but Pinydo lives very far away. I told him to go home. I told him that I would be ok to walk to my house.

I took out 50 South Sudan Pounds and I gave it to him for his transport home and I said goodbye to him. I walked to my house that was about fifteen minutes away from the hospital and on my way going home I received a phone call from one of the high-ranking officers Abraham Simon Makuach.

He worked at the Rajaf National Police College. On my way to my house I began to worry a lot about why Abraham was calling me. He had never called me before. I took my bag home first when I reached home and I put my bag inside my room. I walked outside quickly and my cousin asked me why you walking so fast. She started to worry a lot too as I told her I would come back because I was on my way to meet with Abraham.

I received a lot of phone calls from a lot of my colleagues telling me that the college principal and Abraham were looking for me. They asked me what happened and what I had done wrong. I told them I don't really know.

I met Abraham at the Step Club opposite Juba University. Abraham told me that he had been given orders by our college principal to call me and that I had to go back to the police training college. It was seven pm at night while I was there with Abraham. He called our college principal and told him on the phone that I was there with him. The college principal sent his driver to come and pick us up.

While we were waiting I asked Abraham what was going on

and why did the college principal want me. He said he didn't really know and that he was given orders by him to call me and he did. He said his driver would tell me about what I did so I said ok. We were waiting for his driver and when he came I got inside the car.

Two people were sitting in the car. A driver and other two police officers wearing their police uniforms and holding their AK47 guns. I was panicking and worried about what I had done wrong. When I was inside the car I asked college principal Atem's driver and his bodyguard what I had done wrong. One of them told me that they were taking me back to the police training college. That's all they told me.

One of the officers called Atem phoned the college principal and told him that I was with them and that they were taking me back to the police college now. Whatever else they said on the phone I didn't hear it.

When we arrived at Rajaf Police Police College, it was 8.30pm and I was taken inside the cell and locked in. The cell was located at the main gate of Police college. I was just inside the cell wondering what I had done wrong.

I was very sick as well. My phone was taken away from me and they told me to remove my belt too and so I did and I handed them to the police members who worked on the main gate. Inside, the cell was too cold with a lot of mosquitoes and lizards running around everywhere.

One of the police officers came and asked me which one was the room I slept in so he could go and bring me a blanket. I told him to also tell my colleagues that I was inside the cell. Most of my colleagues and officers who had heard about it came to see me inside the cell and asked about what I had done wrong. I explained it to them that the college principal was the one who had given the orders to the officers to bring me in here.

They said I would be OK. One of my colleagues who was a friend with me on Facebook mentioned that it could have been because of what I had written on Facebook.

Some of my colleagues who were close friends to me went and rang up my father and told him about the issues between myself and the college principal. My father thought that it was something simple that would end in few days. I slept inside the cell for a good two days. I hadn't heard anything from the college principal about my case and I was feeling sick. It was getting worse day and night until the 28th of June when I was still inside the cell.

One of the police officers who was in charge of the cell reported to the main office about my sickness to high ranking officers. It was around ten am when the college principal sent two police officers including his driver to come and take me to hospital for further treatment. They came holding their guns. They called me to get up. They opened the cell and as I walked outside they told me to get inside the car. I was being mistreated badly. I couldn't go and have shower outside or go to toilet. I was guided around by the police officers carrying their guns in their hands so that if I was to run away they could shoot me. I was being treated like a major criminal.

It was a nightmare to me and I felt so sad being mistreated this way in my own motherland. Sometimes I just sat inside the cell and cred inside my heart with tears coming out of my eyes feeling very sad and worried. I found my life then to be very useless.

On our way to Juba hospital I was sitting in the pickup car and two police sat next to me with their guns. The driver was driving very fast on the road dodging the many potholes. One of the police officers on top of the vehicle fell down hitting his head onto the rocks. He was bleeding badly as driver stopped on the side of the road. We all assisted to pick him up. His clothes were bloodied all over.

One female police officer with two stars called the college principal and told him about the situation. We drove back to the police college with the injured officer. I saw the college principal walking toward the car and he started to yell at the driver. I was just sitting in the vehicle worried about my case. The college principal took out some money and gave it to the bleeding officer and sent us off to the hospital for treatment.

The officer was bleeding a lot. I took out my hand cloth from my belt and I gave it to him to cover his wounds. Around eleven forty-five am we arrived at the Atlabara hospital. It is one of the busiest hospitals and was connected with the Police College as well. Our papers were given to the doctors and we waited in the waiting area.

I was taken to different room and the officer was taken to the operation theatre for surgery to his head and knees. I was given injections for malaria as well as malaria medicine. All our treatments cost about 7000 South Sudanese Pounds. It is a very expensive hospital. After our treatment we drove back to the police training college.

I was taken back to the cell and given my treatment medicines to take while I was inside until Thursday the 30th of June 2016. It was around nine am when I was called to the office about my case. I was being charged for what I wrote on Facebook on the 23rd of June 2016.

Chapter 18

I was arrested on the 30th of June. I was interviewed by a police officer who was given orders to interview me about what I wrote on Facebook. He asked whether I had written this on Facebook and I said yes I did and that the reason I wrote it was because of the situations I had seen in this country. I saw street children and innocent people who didn't have fathers or uncles working in government struggling in the country. This was why I wrote it.

Then they told me that I was a cadet and was not allowed to write anything concerning politics on social media. I told them it was my opinion. On that day I was charged and I was to be taken to Juba Central Prison for two months and then dismissed from the police training college.

On the same day I was taken to prison before we left the college with the college principal's driver and his bodyguards and one of the police officers with one star. I asked the police officer if I could use his phone to call my dad to tell him about it.

My father told me to give the phone to the officer. He talked to him and after they talked the officer gave the phone back to me and I spoke to my father. He told me to meet him at the front gate of the prison. My phone and belt was given to the officer for holding.

Upon reaching the prison's main gate my father and my uncle Leek Manyang were there already waiting for us. When we got out from the car and before I stepped inside prison my father spoke to me. I remember his words very well.

The Reflection of my Journey to the Republic of South Sudan

He said to me "Manyang, don't worry about being locked up in prison. This is what a man can face and stay strong in prison."

I looked at him and I cried and then I went inside. When prisoners go into prison in South Sudan the officers make people kneel down and interview them. My papers were given to the prison's administrations office.

They read it. One of the officers told the college principal's driver that a cadet cannot be locked up in prison. They denied me entry to be in prison and the college principal's driver called the police college's administrations office. He told him that the prison officers refused to let me into prison.

Then the college principal rang up the Director General of Prisons told him to let this cadet into the prison. The officer then told me that the orders had come from above and that he was sorry and that this country's laws are there but not being followed up and according to the laws I could not be inside prison. But the orders came from above so they would put me inside while waiting for clarification.

I saw a lot of new prisoners waiting to get locked inside. I was told to sit down and I did. I was given a prison uniform and I was taken inside prison. When I stepped into the prison, I saw a lot of prisoners sitting under the tree in the shade. I was taken to a room where I could sleep.

All the prisoners were willing to hear about my case and I told them and they all told me that my case was not that serious. I met with a lot of prisoners who had been in prison for many years without meeting with judges.

Life in South Sudan's prison wasn't that easy. Prisoners were being mistreated. They were often treated like animals by the prison staff. I saw two prison officers coming into our room working with sticks when they arrived in our room. I heard everyone saying "Solo solo". These are the words the prisoners use when officers come inside their room and if you have a phone inside prison with you or money you hide it somewhere that they won't find it.

One of the officers walked towards me and he started to search me. He thought maybe that I had money or a phone. He couldn't find anything and they walked outside going to different rooms searching around all day. That was their job inside prison.

Prisoners were often being beaten and mistreated badly inside Juba Central Prison. To most of the staff the prisoners were useless. Some people do deserve to be inside prison like those who take human lives. The killers, they may deserve it a lot.

Some people however are innocent. They may have been arrested by police from the streets or been locked up by high ranking officers because the country's laws were not being respected. There were people who had been arrested and sent to prison for stealing goats, cattle, or having borrowed money from people and been unable to pay them back. They were being arrested and sentenced to prison and may stay there over one year or more.

During my first week inside prison I was stressed. I started to blame myself more for coming to South Sudan. To be in a country where the laws were not being followed or respected by police and other forces. A country where people were being mistreated and treated like animals. Sometimes I sat down and thought too much about the time I wasted in South Sudan. I blamed myself most of the time.

While in prison I saw a lot of people with mental illnesses. In prison they were not being helped at all. About two weeks later I began to be a counsellor in prison counselling a lot of the prisoners. I sometimes sat down with them and I started to advise them and share my stories with them. I told them how good Australia was and they were interested to hear a lot of stories about Australia. Every day I was surrounded by a lot of prisoners. I became talkative and entertaining to the prisoners. Everyone started to like me. I began to be well known in prison by prisoners. I made a lot of friends with them.

While in prison I was very sick with malaria and the stress was annoying me too much. My life inside prison was better compared with other prisoners who didn't have fathers or relatives outside to support them in like bringing food, changing clothes or medicines when they were sick. My father he was always there for me. He never gave up on me.

Every Thursday, Friday and Saturday from seven am to five pm. These were the days visitors were allowed to visit prisoners in Juba Central Prison. My colleagues and family always came on these days to visit me. I never felt lonely during my time in prison. Sometimes I did just feel stressed thinking of the times I wasted at Police College during the heavy training and being dismissed from Police college.

After all it was because of what I wrote on Facebook about feeding the street children. South Sudan police were not being respected by the higher-ranking police officers. They abused the laws to mistreat people instead of protecting them. They were beating them up and treating all of them badly unlike what I see of the Victoria Police or Australia Police. Australian Police are there to protect everyone. At least if you committed crimes that broke the laws that was when you got arrested. I wish those procedures were followed in my motherland South Sudan.

During my time in Juba Central Prison I have seen horrible situations. One day after I had spent two weeks in prison, I saw a man who had been in prison for over ten years. His case was never followed up by his family. He found himself lonely and one day he got so sick of that prison life of being in one place for over ten years, that he put a rope around his neck and climbed up on top of the tree and jumped. All the prisoners and prison officers went to the place to see the guy hanging up on top of the tree. It was my first time in my life that I saw this kind of insanity. All the prisoners were mourning and feeling very sad. His family were called afterward to take his body.

Prison officers were not equal. Some treated prisoners like dogs and some could treat you with dignity. The majority of the prison officers were not educated. Those who were educated seemed to treat prisoners as equals. The uneducated seemed to just work without any knowledge of human behavior. This is why the prison is very demeaning in South Sudan.

Every night in prison all the prisoners pray in every room. In prison at night prisoners perform church songs singing loudly and praying loudly before everyone sleeps.

While in prison my father and my relatives started to follow up my case outside to assist me to be released from prison. The police college principal who sent me to prison told my father while in prison that he was punishing me for writing on Facebook and for feeding street children. And that when I got out of prison, he would take me back to police college and continue with my police training. My father was about to appeal and the college principal told him not to appeal my case. My father believed in him and he did not write the appeal letter. My uncle who was one of the highest generals in the South Sudan army named Mariel Chanoung and my father together wrote an apology letter on behalf of me to the college principal. He refused to accept this letter. The Inspector General of the South Sudan Police asked him to return me back to Police College and he refused this as well.

While in prison I met one of my childhood friends after twelve years without seeing each other. Unbelievably, we were meeting inside prison. We sat down at every spare moment and shared our childhood memories and stories. I was so happy to meet him again but we were meeting in the wrong place.

Juba Central Prison was established in 1931 when Ahboud

The Reflection of my Journey to the Republic of South Sudan

was then the president of the Republic of Sudan. More than 11,000 inmates have been executed by hanging in Juba prison alone since 1934 up to 2005. In the secession of South Sudan from Sudan, thirty one inmates were executed by hanging until 2015 when South Sudan abolished hanging and resorted to life sentences in prison.

Juba central prison is characterized into 3 departments:

A. Condemned inmates departments.
B. Convicted inmates departments, both short sentences and life imprisonment.
C. Romance inmates departments.

Prison feeding included one meal per day and no medicines. Inmates died quickly from curable diseases like malaria, typhoid and tuberculosis.

Prison accommodations were 15 wards for all inmates and 2 wards for inmates with mental disorders. The prison opened at seven am and closed at five pm and had a tall wall and security fence around it. No one was allowed to go outside the prison without authorization and the water and sanitation services were very poor. There was a cholera epidemic that no treatment was provided for and inmates died every year.

There are more than 1700 inmates and there were 150 men and women on duty daily as prison officers. Religious exercise was free but several things were not allowed in prison including: phones, case money, cigarettes, beer wall, knives, firearms, fire and fish or bone meat. Cooking and perfume was allowed but any fish or bone meat brought to you by your family was confiscated and eaten by the prison officers.

Inmates are not allowed to stand when the officers on duty arrive and instead you are told to kneel down. The administrative structure at the prison level is headed by the Director of Prison and the Deputy Director. The female inmates departments are headed by a major or captain.

More than 1,000 detainees were at the prison, including 119 inmates on death row and others who have not been tried in court. Diseases have mainly affected those awaiting trials.

There were areas with a lot of problems. Certain diseases appeared which caused swelling of the legs, stomach and the eyelids.

The ministry of health is not doing anything about these situations.

In Juba Central Prison some suspects were being held on minor charges without trial.

There were also many inmates whose cases have not been heard in court since they were taken to prison.

If you were being taken inside to wait on a trial you were unreasonably jailed because there were so many cases to deal with. It is not fair but because of poor management they just do it.

Some of those cases could have been handled by police instead of jailing them.

Some of these cases are minor ones but people were brought in and detained in prison. These cases were supposed to be handled by the police but instead they were often brought to prison.

Chapter 20

One day while in Juba Central prison I was visited by one of my colleagues who brought three hundred South Sudanese Pounds with him. A prison officer was standing beside me when he saw me taking money from my colleague but he didn't said anything about it. When my colleague left and I was going back inside our room he call me very loudly with a rude voice. I turned around looking at him with serious eyes trying to scare him. He walked towards me and he started to search me, and when he found the money in my pocket, he tried to take it.

I held his hands very tightly, pushed him and I yelled at him very loudly. The other prison officers came running toward us with sticks trying to scare me. I was not scared at all. I was sick and tired of them mistreating prisoners badly all the time. I told them I was not letting him go with my money. I needed this money. It belonged to me.

More officers turned up and they started to push me hard. I was very strong for them and one of the prison officers hit me with sticks and then he tried a second time and I pulled the sticks from him. I was about to hit him back and he ran away.

I heard one of the prison officers screaming loudly for help more than five times. I pushed one of them and he fell down to the ground. He got up screaming loudly. I started to laugh at these weak officers. I still held the money on my pocket and they tried to get it. I was being surrounded by a lot of officers and I was in the middle. I looked for the weakest side I could take to get out from the middle of them. They were all targeting the money I had in my pocket so they could take it.

I took out the money and I show it to them and I ripped the notes into such small pieces thatl they all became mad at me. They started to beat me up badly and I was taken to the administration office for a further interview.

One of the high ranking officers with three stars was a very respectful officer. I had never met him in prison but all the prisoners respected him and he interviewed me about this issue of money and why I ripped up this money. One of the prisoners named Amad Omar also defended me. The case went really well. He told me not to do it again and the next day the captain of the prison called my father and explained to him what had happened. My father was disappointed with me asking me why I had done that when I was a prisoner and not allowed to bring money into prison. I apologized to my father and to the captain as well.

I was taken back inside the prison leaving my father and officers talking in the office. The case was talked out between my father and officers and I wrote a small letter to the captain as an apology about what I did to his staff and he accepted my apology letter. Being a prisoner was stressful and painful. You cannot do what you like and you don't have freedom as a prisoner and you do what the officers tell you to do.

Chapter 21

On the 1st of August 2016 after two months I was released from prison. That day I woke up very early in the morning before officers opened the doors to let prisoners out.

I told one of the prison officers who was in charge that day to check my name on the list of people who were going to be released on that day. He had the list with him and he checked it and my name was on the list so he told me to pack all my clothes and by midday I would be out of prison.

It was seven am and I started to feel happy. I took all my clothes except what I was wearing and I gave them to other prisoners who had to stay in prison for years including my bed sheets and pillow. I was just sitting outside under the tree waiting for noon to come. The time was passing by slowly.

When the time came the officers came with a list and called the names out of those who were going to be released. I was one of them and we walked outside. The other prisoners came to say their goodbyes to us. When I stepped outside, I was very happy to see the fresh air outside and feel new again.

My father saw me and he started to smile and feel happy too. We both felt happy. My life in the Juba Central Prison was a life experience.

On our way home, my father took me to a local restaurant to eat. Finally, I was outside and eating healthy food. I ordered dry fish, the food I loved most in South Sudan.

While in the restaurant with my father I caught a look at his face and I cried. I said to him: "I just want to say thank you dad, you have been up and down because of me, coming to visit me in prison every week." and the words were really hard to come out.

Again I started to cry. He looked at me and told me to take it easy. I wiped my face, washed my hands and we ate together. I was feeling happy to share food with my father and talk at the table. My father is a great man.

Afterwards we left and went home to where we live in the area called Sherrikat. It was one of the quiet areas my father moved to when I was in prison. It was a very nice place. I have a lot of friends and families living around that area.

One week after I got out of prison, my father and I went to the Police Training College to see the college principal. On our way there I was just thinking too much about all the hard life I had been through while in South Sudan.

When we reached the main gate of the Police College, I saw the cell I was locked in for a week. This was when I was arrested before I was taken to Juba Central Prison. It reminded me again of the hardship I faced during the time I was in that cell and I felt sad about it.

When I reached the office of the college principal all my former colleagues saw me. They walked towards me calling my name happily. They all felt happy to see me again. They were worried about me while I was in prison.

I remained outside and my father went in to see the college principal. They talked about my case and the college principal had told my father that when I got out from prison he would return me to the Police Training College to finish up my training and law classes was what he had said.

He hadn't followed it up and it seemed like he was a man who wouldn't keep his word. He was a leader with a lot of stars on his shoulders and leading half of the country and so it disappointed me that he would not keep his word.. He refused to return me to college and he dismissed me. My father walked outside feeling disappointed at what the college principal had told him.

We left to go back home. Some of my colleagues started to call me on my phone and ask me if I was returning to the college. I told them that the college principal had refused and most of them expressed sadness and said sorry. They told me on the phone that I was still their colleague and that they would never forget me.

One of my colleagues came to my house to say he was sorry about my dismissal from the Police college and to tell me to stay strong. He said that police work was not the only key to open a door and that I could do different work and survive like others and not to think about this too much.

His words was very strong and helpful and that kept me strong. I still caught up with some of my colleagues and some of the officers from police training college who were close friends to me including officers Jackson Mayiik Chol Guot, Farwel James and Mosaad Altom. We caught up sometimes over the weekend and had coffee together. Some officers and cadets were not happy about my dismissal from Police Training College.

The names of the people who came and visited me during the time I was in prison are these lovely people:

My father Enock Malet Manyang
My mother Abuk Chagai Matet
My brother Thon Malet Manyang
My brother Mayen Malet Manyang
My first cousin Maburuk Agorrok
My first cousin Achol Aborish Arou
My sister Achol Malet Manyang
My cousin Leek
My colleague Leek Garang Leek

South Sudan 2015–2017

My colleague Garang Mabior
My colleague Michael Mayen Arol
My colleague Pinydo Majak Barkuei
My colleague Majur Ayoor
My colleague Edward Loro
My friend and he was one of our best law teacher at the police college Jackson Mayiik Chol Guot
My cousin Riak Deng

Some of my colleagues and families lived very far away and couldn't make it to visit me in prison but they sent their greetings to me via my colleagues and family who always came and visited me in prison.

South Sudan's prison population of approximately 1,700 have mostly not been convicted of any offense or in some cases even charged with one, but are detained, often for long periods, waiting for police, prosecutors, and judges to process their cases.

The vast majority of detainees have no legal representation, because they cannot afford a lawyer and South Sudan has no functioning legal aid system at all. Judges pass long sentences and even condemn to death people who, without legal assistance, were unable to understand the nature of charges against them or to call and prepare witnesses in their defense.

Frustration with, and confusion about, the criminal justice system are common among prisoners. I have stayed in the Juba Central Prison for two months and have observed a lot of the prisoners never getting to see a judge. The court has not called for their cases. The Attorney General doesn't follow the law. The police often don't abide by the law and they work for their benefit and use the prisoners a lot. Inmates do not get enough to eat and prison water is also in short supply. Prisoners are vulnerable to illness and disease, and when they fall sick, they rarely receive proper care, unless they can pay for the medicine themselves or their families can bring medicines to them in prison.

A lot of inmates died in the South Sudan prison and I have witnessed it. I always worried that I would be the next person to die. Inmates got beaten by prison workers with sticks, canes or whips for disciplinary infractions. Some inmates are permanently chained in heavy shackles. This violates domestic and international standards for the use of restraints. This also constitutes prohibited, cruel, inhuman, and degrading punishment. Children are also detained alongside adults and are not offered rehabilitation programs or sufficient educational opportunities, as required under South Sudan's Child Act.

Chapter 22

After I got out of prison on the 1th of August 2016 I never heard anything from the Police college principal about my case again. I decided to return to Australia. Before I came back, I enjoyed my last holidays with my family and friends in Juba telling them that I would be going back to Australia soon.

Some said to make sure you come back and don't stay away from your motherland too long. Even though you were mistreated by the government make sure you come back. South Sudan systems will change one day and you can work again in your motherland. Hearing these words from my friends and family made me feel happy a lot. I had made my decision not to return to South Sudan again but when I heard these words it made me feel happy so I feel like going back again in the future.

I went to a place called Nimule to visit my uncle's family when I got out from prison. Nimule is about two hours away from Juba and a very small town. It's near the border between South Sudan and Uganda. This was the place my uncle Leek Manyang lived in with his family.

It was my second time in Nimule. I enjoyed my holiday there with my uncle's family, and I used to go to a river called the Anyama river. I woke up every morning and went there after I had breakfasted each day. I took my uncle's son Mayen Leek with me and sat under the tree where we could see the other side of river.

There we could see cattle keepers walking around with their cattle. They could be heard singing traditional songs while walking around with their cattle. It was a very nice view and we normally spent two hours just walking around the riverbank. Anyama river is one of the famous rivers in the Nimule area and in all of South Sudan.

After enjoying my two weeks holiday with my uncle's family I had lasting memories of Nimule. I came back to Juba and on my way from Nimule to Juba I met with one of my childhood friends that I hadn't seen for over fifteen years. I met him on the bus when we were coming to Juba. I was sitting in the middle of the bus seat and he was behind me.

When his phone rang with nice traditional music for a ringtone I turned around and I told him "Nice music, brother."

He looked at me and he screamed very loud "Manyang, is that you, Manyang Malet?"

I said "It's me, Manyang."

The bus was running on the road and everyone turned around and looked at us. I gave him a big hug. We were very happy to see each other after years.

We continued our journey going to Juba and we swapped seats with one of the passengers to talk together. I went to the back seat and we sat together with my childhood friends. Our journey was good as the Nimule Highway was one of the developed roads in South Sudan.

About two hours later we arrived in Juba. We got out from the vehicle and walked to the nearest restaurant. We had lunch together and a cup of tea. He started to ask me some questions like when I had come to South Sudan. When I told him that I had been in Juba for two and half years he couldn't believe it. I told him about my time in South Sudan.

Then he told me that South Sudan had still not finalised or implemented all the laws yet. The law was not well respected and he was very sorry about my experiences. Before we said goodbye to each other I told him that I would go back to Australia and that sometime soon we could meet again upon my return in the future if we were still alive.

He told me to go say hello to all my family in Australia and thank god that we met again after these long years apart. He said people can meet if they are alive and it's only the mountains that they never meet. Then afterwards we washed our hands and he left.

I stood in one place for just a few minutes looking at him walking away until he turned right and disappeared. Then I was left with the happy memories of seeing my childhood friend again.

He and I used to go to childcare together back in 1995 in Kakuma Refugee Camp and stayed together in the refugee camp until we separated in 2005.

Chapter 23

When I came back from Nimule to Juba I stayed for a few weeks and prepared myself for my last visit to Bor Town. I needed to say goodbye to my family and friends that live in Bor Town.

On Thursday the 19th of November 2016 myself and my older brother Thon Malet Manyang and our cousin Magai Daau Lual left Juba at around eleven am to go to Bor. The driver's name was Chol. I couldn't remember his dad's name but he is a cool dude. He is best friends with my older brother Thon Malet.

Our main mission was to say goodbye to my friends and families who live in Bor Town and go and visit my grandmother Adhieu Mayom Ayiik's grave for the first time. This had been my plan for a very long-time. Even before I went to South Sudan, I always wanted to visit my grandmother's grave.

When we left Juba going to Bor Town we ran into some peacekeeper patrols along a notoriously dangerous road between Juba and Bor. In the neighbouring Jonglei region, peacekeepers enable people and goods to travel safely again.

Most people have no option but to travel via this road because the cost of flying is out of reach at 10-12,000 South Sudanese pounds a trip which is about two years' salary for the average South Sudanese public servant.

On my last day of traveling to Bor Town, two days before I left Juba on the 16th of November 2016 there was a heavy gunfight that took place along the Juba-Bor road around 10am and lasted for about two hours. The sporadic sounds of both light and heavy machine guns were heard by people in the residences of Juba. It started at around 10am and lasted for about two hours. It was not clear which groups were involved in the gunfight.

However later on in the morning the government army brought several wounded and dead people to the Juba Military hospital.

Nobody claimed any responsibility. However, some people with knowledge of the security sector said the government soldiers were firing at people believed to be from the Murle ethnic group. Possibly they were escaping from Juba to Boma. But this could not be confirmed.

As a result of this the Army and Police were on the Bor and Juba road patrolling around the main areas. We left on the 19th of November. The car we used was a pickup vehicle and we sat on top with almost thirty people.

I was worried about any possible gunfire again and I silently began to pray whilst on top of vehicle. I prayed quietly for our journey to be successful. The Juba - Bor Town road was still the same. Nothing had changed since I had travelled on this road in December 2014. There were still too many holes in the road. Nothing had changed at all.

As we continued our journey we started to talk. We shared some stories around and my brother Thon was holding my camera and taking photos on the road. I was not sitting comfortably on the vehicle. My body was not relaxed at all and I worried too much about the recent gunfire that I had heard about on this road.

In our vehicle I saw two army men traveling with us wearing their army uniforms and carrying their guns with them. We continued our journey and all the passengers were very worried about the insecurity on the road. On our way we saw government army personnel sitting under the tree with heavy machine guns protecting people while they were traveling to Bor Town.

I gave my brother Thon Malet my camera to take pictures on

The Reflection of my Journey to the Republic of South Sudan

the road. It was too hot and we were burning badly plus there were dust storms on the road. I began to feel sick feeling like I wanted to vomit. I was feeling dizzy and my nose was blocked.

All the army war tanks were still on the roadside. After we drove for almost one hour on the road we came to the bush where we could not see any houses and only trees and mountains. The driver and two passengers who were sitting in the front seat saw two guys on the road carrying guns crossing the road ahead with their cattle. They were cattle keepers.

The driver wiped down the mirror and he raised his voice up calling my brother Thon's name. Then Thon asked who these people carrying the guns coming out from the bush were. The driver was about to stop and my brother told him to continue driving. He did so and was panicking all the passengers including myself. The two army guys we were with started to prepare themselves positioning and holding their guns properly ready for action.

We passed through and they just looked at us. They didn't say anything but they tried to scare us with their guns. It was likely that they were scared too when seeing our two soldiers with us with their guns ready loaded with bullets. The journey was too long.

When we reached the Mangala area I got off from the vehicle and walked around. The driver said we would spend half an hour in Mangala. It reminded me of a lot of stories of Mangala from the first time when I passed by while going to Bor Town on my first visit in December 2014.

Most of the shops were closed. Only a few were still working. The first restaurant I had eaten in on my first journey there was closed as well. The cattle keepers had moved away from the riverside to a place further along. A lot of things had changed in Mangala.

I asked one of the shopkeepers what had happened to a lot of shops and restaurants in here. He told me that most of them were closed down due to financial issues. Things had become very expensive in Juba so they could not afford to rent and buy things from Juba to send here as it involved expensive transportation.

About half an hour later we left to get back to our vehicle and continue our journey. My body was still not feeling well when we left. Twenty minutes later on the road I began to feel my head spin and ache too. I tried to speak up but I couldn't. I was very sick and powerless.

While the vehicle was moving the sun was getting too hot and my body was becoming very hot too. I fell down from the top of the vehicle while the vehicle was running at an 80 kph speed on the difficult road.

Everyone began to yell, telling the driver to stop so the driver did. They all got out from the vehicle and began running towards me. I was completely flat on the ground and I couldn't breathe properly and my body began to shake on the ground. I could hear people's voices after five or so minutes. My brother started to pour water on me.

I opened my eyes and everyone asked me if I was ok. I tried to respond to them but couldn't. My voice was too low. I just nodded my head. I saw my brother dropping tears calling my name very loudly I just looked at him and I couldn't respond. He took out his phone trying to call our father but the network was bad. We were in the bush where there was no network at all.

My last journey to my village was turning out very badly. I cannot remember much about this journey as it started badly and ended badly.

After a few minutes I got up from the ground but I was powerless and my brother and cousin started to pull me up more and support me as I walked to the car. The guy who was sitting in the front seat told me to sit in his seat and we continued the journey from there.

My body was paining a lot and a headache was annoying me too. I started to cry and I heard driver saying apologisingand I told him it was OK.

Around 7pm we finally arrived in Bor Town after all this mess on the road. We alighted from the vehicle and my brother Thon started to argue with one of the passengers who was complaining about the car delay on the road. He was worried about the car being delayed on the road but not about a sick person. That's when my brother got sad and started to argue. I had to separate them.

Afterwards my brother called my father and told him about it and my father began to worry. He told Thon to pass the phone to me. I spoke to him and he sound very worried on the phone. I told him I would be OK and that we were walking to a local clinic now to get.

My brother Thon and I and our cousin Magai walked to a local clinic still not feeling well. The clinic we walked into belonged to my cousin's doctor Chaw Mayol Juuk. This clinic was just on the main road not far from Bor Town close to the main market place. My father continued calling my brothers phone every half an hour. I was given good treatment by Doctor Chaw Mayol. We then left at about nine pm in the hot weather.

We walked into a motel but I cannot remember the name of it. We rented three rooms, one for each of us. My brother and my cousin left and I remained in the motel to sleep as my body was hurting and tired from this long journey. I slept from ten pm until I woke up the next day at two pm. I had turned off my phone and locked my room while sleeping.

My dad and the rest of my cousins had been calling me while my phone was off. When I woke up and turned on my phone I could see 35 missed calls and I had to call them back again. They were all worried about me and I told them that I was ok and feeling a bit better. My father never stopped calling. I even got tired of picking up his calls because he had been calling so much.

The 22nd of November 2016 was a big day in my life. I visited my uncles that I had never met before. Around ten am we went to a black-market money exchange. I had two hundred USD.

It's always an interesting process in South Sudan. I got the number of the guy who exchanged USD. into South Sudanese Pounds. Before you exchange money you first have to contact someone who has a contact in the market that is trusted. Then they check the exchange rate to see if it is reasonable. Then we go to their shop.

The shops are on dirt streets as there are no paved roads in Bor Town, though it is the Capital of Jonglei State. It is a tent like structure and some have corrugated metal sides and a roof.

The one we went to on that day was a shop that sold clothes, shoes, suitcases, toys, furniture and plastic containers, kind of like a small Wal-Mart. You make a connection with the owner and then go to a secluded area of the shop. The owner takes out a bag from underneath some shelves. He counts the amount of money we wanted to change and then counts out the South Sudanese Pounds to give in exchange. Most of the time we receive the bills in denominations of 10, 20, 25 or 50 SSP. Only once have we received 100 SSP bills.

That day we exchanged 500 USD for our trip to Bor Town we received 24.000 SSP. It is hard to imagine how big a pile of money that is. The owner then lets you borrow a bag or suitcase big enough to fit all the money you have changed. We then took that money back to the hotel and put it in my backpack. Then at some point we took the borrowed bag back to the owner.

My cousin and I and my older brother Thon then went and visited my uncles that we used to hear about. They are from my mother's side and the rest of my family. When we met them they welcomed us and I started to cry. I was so happy to meet them for the first time in my life. We sat down under a tree in the shade and talked.

I asked one of the elders to take us to my grandmother Adhieu Mayom Ayiik's grave. She passed away in 2008. They said ok and we did a short prayer together with over ten elders, two youths and four women amongst all my relatives. After half an hour we walked to my grandmother's grave. She was buried at my Aunty Arual's house. I started to remember all good things she used to for us. At her graveside I cried and my aunty told me to stop crying and we had a short prayer at her graveside. Then I took a picture of my grandmother's grave.

We sat inside the room made out of mud. We started to talk to my aunty and we were very happy to see each other after seventeen years away from each other. My aunty had a lot of cattle at her house.

We walked outside with my camera and I took photos of her cattle. There were over 60 cattle. My Aunty Arual brought traditional milk and our traditional food. We ate it and drank our traditional milk. It was the best day in my life.

Her children came and sat next to us. We started to talk and they asked me about Australian life. They were very interested in hearing more about it. Three hours later I told aunty that we were leaving and she told us to stay longer but we had to go and meet other family members and friends. She said ok and before we left I took out 1000 South Sudanese Pounds and gave it to her. I took pictures of her and her children for memories and we said our goodbyes to her.

We went back to our hotel and it was three pm and we left feeling happy. Bor Town was good, life was really great in my village and everyone was very friendly. We went to the Marol market every night to shop. The market continues till ten pm at night so we would sit outside and have tea. The Police, Army and National Security patrol both day and night to make Bor Town safe. We walked safely at night unlike Juba where there were a lot of unknown gunmen shooting at people randomly.

On the 28th of November, one week later, my father got me an airline ticket. I was not to travel back to Juba by road. I travelled in a small aeroplane as my father worried about how I had fallen down from the vehicle on the trip to Bor Town. He got me an airline ticket and paid 100 USD for it. My father cared a lot about me.

My brother and my cousin travelled to Juba by car using the same road. We went to Bor Town airport. When we reached there my brother argued with one of the workers at there. The guy was very rude to us and we nearly had a fight with him. I pulled my brother aside and I told him to calm down and he did. I checked in and I got into the plane.

When we landed at Juba International Airport my father was waiting for me. I saw my dad and he started to laugh and I gave him a hug and I thanked him for getting me a ticket to come back by aeroplane. He said it was ok then we walked to a place where he parked his car and he took me home.

Chapter 24

We got ready for Christmas which was just around the corner. I stayed in Juba waiting to celebrate the last Christmas holidays with my family before I returned to Australia during the first week of December.

I decided to go to the Juba Military Hospital. I never gave up on helping poor people. When I arrived and walked around checking every room in the hospital I saw a lot of wounded soldiers who had got shot in war zones or had been in accidents on the roads. They were laying down on their beds feeling sick and struggling from their wounds. I spent more than two hours just talking with them and heard a lot of very sad stories. I walked outside feeling sad and when I arrived home and sat down with my father, I told him about my visit to the hospital. He was happy to hear about it and I asked him what I could buy for people who were shot and wounded. He told me to buy them soaps.

On the 5th of December 2016 I went to Konyo Knoyo market which is one of the largest markets in South Sudan. Konyo Konyo Market is a busy trading hub where you can buy almost anything you want: food items, vegetables, fruits, clothing items, and many others. Boys were playing ball, women were selling small bags of sugar or charcoal, children were selling plastic bottles of milk and cooks were dropping dough balls into hot oil. There were dogs on every corner and hardware shops selling shiny pots and electrical cords. There were hookah shops, tailors, and bakers.

I bought eight boxes of soaps and a few bedsheets and I took them to the Juba Military Hospital as part of my donation to the country and the poor people in hospital. I never gave up on helping my people.

There were a lot of wounded people in the hospital, over 300 people and they were all suffering. They needed a lot of help. The doctors and wounded people were very happy with what I did and I became well known.

It made me well respected by a lot of South Sudanese people from Australia and other western countries. They began to call me and compliment me over the mobile phone and Facebook. They sent me money through Amal Express and Dahabshill banks, and some sent 100 USD or more so I could help people in the hospital and street children as well. I was interviewed by the Australian SBS dinka radio network and a lot of people heard of me and my stories through SBS. They began to send me more money to help and I helped a lot of people.

I did that for over two months. The saddest part was that most of these wounded soldiers had families and some were married and some were unmarried. The majority of them stayed in hospital for over a year struggling and I became too stressed. I wanted to help all of them but I had financial issues. The money I had was not enough at all. Helping street children and people with disabilities in hospital was not easy and involved a lot of challenges. Doctors were working hard to save their lives and they worked day and night without a rest.

My life in South Sudan was not easy at all. There was too much stress that I didn't even worry about my life, I worried about the poor people in South Sudan. Life was hard there and my life wasn't easy at all. The whole journey was full of sadness =.

While I was helping wounded people in hospital, one of the doctors Malaak Dit came to me and said he appreciated the work I been doing. He introduced me to one of the young men named

The Reflection of my Journey to the Republic of South Sudan

Peter Ayuen Lueth. Peter Ayuen is a South Sudanese soldier. He got shot a lot of times in different areas and wounded.

Peter Ayuen Lueth was born in 1976 in Jale Payam Aboudit clan, the second child amongst four girls and three boys. He married Aluel Deng Magot Anok Ateng and had four children: Atong Peter Ayuen, Akoi Peter Ayuen, Lueth Peter Ayuen and Aduot Peter Ayuen.

During the civil war they fled to Ethiopia in 1987. The minors stayed in a refugee camp and later got drafted by the army and graduated with Intisar two. He was in survival mode and he never gave up but things became worse when he heard about the death of his sisters, brothers and his parents who were all killed in the 1991 Jonglei State genocide. He was first shot in Damadola Ethiopia in 1991 but survived and was shot in Magui in 1992, Kapoeta in 1994, Ngangala in 1999, and Raja in 2001. He was shot multiple times again in Malakal 2006 wounding both his legs. He was air lifted by the Red Cross to the Juba Teaching Hospital where he spent seven years and moved to a different hospital because of treatment complications.

He spent seven and half years in the Juba Teaching Hospital to recover and in 2013 went to the civil war. A lot of people were also killed there and some fled to refugee camps and some were IDPs. He was still in the hospital and when the people broke into the hospital and started shooting a lot of patients were also killed. He was unfortunately shot again four times in the crossfire. He has been shot a total of twenty times during the civil war and even after the comprehensive peace agreement. Some of the bullets have been removed and some are still in his body.

He really needs a lot of help as both of his legs have now been amputated. He believes he can still live his life with joy and take care of his family.

He believes that God has a purpose for him and that is why he is still alive today. He is currently seeking a wheelchair because he believes it would help him work to help his children, wife and move around. A wheelchair costs about $700 to $2000. Anything would definitely help him and his family. Life in South Sudan is very hard even for those who are not disabled.

Peter Ayuen Lueth Nai introduced me to a young man named Bol Jombo Magany who was born in 1987 in Goi in Pariak in Bor Town. He was shot and would on the 20th of February 2014 in Malakal in the Upper Nile. He is married with two girls and two boys and lost his six brothers in the war between the government and the rebels in Bor Town in 2013. He lives with one sister and a brother named Malth Jombo Magany and is now paralysed in his lower limbs.

He is from Division Eight and I used to help all of them and I still support them.

Most doctors have left the Juba Military Hospital for private hospitals due to low and pay and the lack of accommodation, work allowances, treatment and travel allowances and the lack of equipment and theatre materials for operations. Patients face risks such as a lack of rehabilitation centres and transportation from where they are wounded to healthcare facilities.

When wounded people are taken to hospital, they are given treatment for 24 hours after which they have to manage on their own. The hospital is struggling to find food and has poor hygiene inside because they don't have co-patient finance so patients often die no matter what.

99.9% of wounded patients who were treated in this hospital lack next of kin to take care of their discharge. Patients rather go back to the market and hotels to get their daily bread because no one in the government will take care of them. Patients can end up dying up in here or go back in the hotels often going mentally insane.

My life in South Sudan was full of sadness seeing these people suffering.

Chapter 25

I am south Sudanese born. I reside in Australia and have been there for several years working. I am a citizen of Australia with firsthand refugee. I was a refugee in Kakuma Refugee camp in Northern Kenya from 1993-2005. Oxfam, UNHCR, and the Red Cross were there supporting us with food and water and other things. I was able to go to school and grow, but at the back of my mind I knew what I wanted to do with my life. I wanted to be able to help those who were in the same situation that I had once been.

While living in different countries and returning to South Sudan I helped vulnerable people and was recruited into police training. I knew I was making a difference in my motherland, even though it was small, in the same way someone had made a difference for me.

Around the time Sudan gained independence, I had the privilege of working with fellow South Sudanese returning home from Australia. There was so much hope. People brought with them dreams and expectations for South Sudan, and for our future. I was so inspired just being with them. Their hope was my hope as well. That seems like a long time ago.

We are now at war, and many of us are lost. Some of us have lost loved ones, and some have been forced to leave their homes. The hope that inspired me is also getting lost. I am a humanitarian because I believe there is still hope for South Sudan. I believe South Sudan is like a guesthouse from God. Peace will come and one day everyone will enjoy the benefit of their motherland South Sudan.

South Sudan 2015–2017

I have the chance to work with communities to discuss issues that we are facing and how to rise above them. I believe that the only way to overcome the challenges we face is to listen to each other and to work together. We need to take the journey to a better future together. The answers are all with us. I wanted to make a difference in people's lives.

I gathered many skills working in the private sector in Australia with Security companies, doing volunteer work with Melbourne's Salvation Army and the Victoria Police. These things have got me thinking that maybe there is more to work than this. I started exploring how my daily work could have a positive effect on others. This is not to say that I wanted to save the world but to make and see some small differences in people's lives.

This work I do helps me to evaluate my own purpose and contribution to the greater good. This is why I enjoy it even now after more than three years in humanitarian work, getting out to the field and being with the people I can support. They are the ones who remind me why I do this work. I belong to a community and that means supporting each other in good and bad times. I started working as a humanitarian to serve the community where I am from. Now I serve any community that needs my help. I help because it is my duty to help others.

I became a humanitarian because I know what it feels like to be in need in South Sudan. I felt it when I was in Police College in Juba and helping street children and people with disabilities. At Police College there were many like me who felt like I did but did not do anything. I feel it now in my heart that many are still suffering. I do what I do because I want to help people in times when they need it the most. I love taking care of people.

I am a child of God. I have experienced war in 2016. There were dead bodies everywhere in Juba. I helped because these people are my community; they are human beings like me. I can't run away from this. You have to be brave and go through it.

People in South Sudan call me a "man of people" because I help the poor people. They know I'm in a similar position as they are and I am helping. This shows a strong sense of equality: that we are all humans and have the same basic ideas about our lives - we all want a home, a safe place to live, and to live in harmony with our neighbor's and nature around us. We all shed tears when we experience sadness or intense joy; when the drums play the beat of our heart, we want to dance. If I can contribute in my own way to create a better future for my fellow humans, I feel human, I feel part of our world, and that more than justifies the changes that I make and how lost I feel sometimes.

I know what it means to be hungry. I know the weakness and desperation you feel when you are hungry. I was in the refugee camp in northern Kenya for fourteen years living as a refugee with my family. I have experienced the life of being hungry in the refugee camp so I can support my fellow brothers and sisters to produce food on their own and be self-sufficient. I feel contented in my heart when I see farmers at the field harvesting their crops, enjoying the fruits after months of cultivation or people milking cows that they have been caring for over many months or even an entire life time.

I decided recently to do what I think every South Sudanese should do in South Sudan. The majority feel that they want to do it too while living in South Sudan. For a good two years, every time I walked on the streets people looked at me as crazy person by the way I walked and the way I acted on the streets. But they never knew that I was doing the duty of care work and studying people who live in South Sudan.

One day, one time I walked into a restaurant and I was wearing a ripped pair of shorts and my feet were full of dust and I looked like a junkie. My baldness made me look like an old man too.

People in that restaurant turned their faces on me and saw me as a junkie.

I saw one of them dressed up in a suit and tie in the temperature of 40 degrees. He looked at me with a smile and nodded his head. I didn't pay attention to them at this point and I sat down and the owner of the restaurant walked toward me and told me to walk outside because I looked like a junkie. I looked at him and I smiled. He felt ashamed as I was laughing at him.

I told him I wanted to eat and to get me a menu. He walked away and then I ordered my food. He asked me to move to the corner which I did. He told me to pay first as he was worried thinking that I will leave without paying. I pulled out a lot of money as I was holding over 10,000 South Sudanese pounds that my friend from Melbourne had sent me. The man was nervous, he tried to apologize to me and he didn't know what to say or how to begin.

After I ate and was about to walk out the guy who was smiling at me said hello. He shook hands proudly and you could see that all of the others felt bad too. At the end they all waved at me when I was leaving. The owner of the restaurant came outside and apologised to me. I told him it was ok and I walked away.

No one is born hating another person because of the color of his skin or his background or his religion. Some people must learn to hate and if they can learn to hate, they can be taught to love, for love comes more naturally to the human heart than its opposite. Never make yourself very special as a lot of South Sudanese do who live in the western world. They often do this when they travel back to Africa. They make themselves very important to their own people as if they came from heaven. Make yourself as a simple person and you will learn a lot. I am proud to be South Sudanese and I am proud to be Australian citizen. Now I am back in Australia living happily with my family.

PART FOUR

Melbourne, Australia

2017 to now

Chapter 26

On the 1st of March 2017 my brother Manyang Malet Manyang got me a return ticket to come back to Australia after I struggled a lot in my motherland South Sudan. I was so excited when he sent me the return ticket. I told my dad early in the morning on the 2nd of March that I would go back to Australia. My dad was happy.

It was both exciting and sad when I told my friends and my former colleagues that I was going back to Australia. A few of them felt bad that I was leaving and that made me sad too to leave them behind. I was busy saying goodbye to a lot of friends in Juba and the saddest part was to leave Ladoli Wani the disabled kid, Peter Ayuen Lueth and Chol Jumbo behind in South Sudan. I had no choice. I also had to leave as my life was being threatened by our police college principal in South Sudan.

My life was sad, very sad in South Sudan. Before I left South Sudan for Australia, I woke up one day and I went to the River Nile in South Sudan. I sat under the mango trees crying and feeling sad and thinking about all my friends that I had met in Juba and Bor Town. Thoughts of leaving them behind were hard to take and I spent almost two hours crying as the water was also flooding and the River Nile was crying with me.

One man was just passing by the River Nile walking towards his house as he lived nearby. He saw me crying and stopped to ask me if I was ok. I said yes, I was and he sat near me and asked me more.

I explained to him all the hardships I had faced in South Sudan. He told me to take it easy and he couldn't leave me behind so he told me to go with him. I got up and we left together. I was very upset and we walked to a tea place where we had more conversation.

Afterwards he left. He went his way and I went to my way. I walked to Ladoli Wani's house to say goodbye to him. I saw Ladoli crawling on the ground at his house as he is a disabled kid and I sat down with him. Saying goodbye to Ladoli was very hard with tears in my eyes. His mother came to me and she wiped my tears away with her clothes and she asked me if I was ok. I told her I was going back to Australia but I was feeling sad to leave Ladoli Wani behind.

She told me it was ok: "You can leave South Sudan as it is not good for you. You have struggled a lot here and you will meet Ladoli again."

Before I left, I took out 2000 South Sudanese Pounds and I gave it to him. I said goodbye and I took his picture with his mother before leaving.

I went to the Juba Military Hospital and said my goodbyes to Peter Ayuen Lueth and Chol Jumbo. One of the hardest parts was saying goodbye to these lovely people that I had met in South Sudan.

On the 3rd of March 2017 I woke up early in the morning and had my last breakfast with my family. I was excited to come back to Australia again after two years away. I was feeling sad too to leave South Sudan behind. I packed all my clothes and took out the belt that my father gave me as a gift in 2005 when I was coming to Australia for the first time. I showed it to my father and I told him I would keep it forever. He was happy with that and I put it into the suit jacket that I was wearing.

Afterwards we left going to the airport. My mother Abuk Chagai, my father Malet Manyang and my uncle James Leek Manyang were going together with me to Juba International Airport. On our way I received a phone call from one of my friends Mayiik Chol Guot. He was my former teacher at the police college and he wanted to say goodbye to me as he couldn't make it to the airport.

When we arrived at Juba International Airport I met with my former colleagues, Leek Garang Leek, Pinydo Majak Barkuei, Majur Ayoor. They were at the airport already preparing to say goodbye to me. We all walked together to the checking area. By the time I checked in it was one pm and my flight was two thirty pm. Before that we took pictures for the memories. I cried many tears leaving these groups of people behind. I took out my passport and it was stamped. My father paid 50 USD. for a departure tax out of Juba. I had a very nice conversation with friends and families at the airport before I took off.

At 2:30pm I got on an Egyptian airline and was seated in the middle seat. There were only a few people traveling to Egypt on that day. My flight was a connecting airline from Juba International Airport to Egypt and then to Dubai. I saw my family standing at the airport waving at me. I was crying while in the aeroplane as we took off. Egypt was about two hours away from Juba and the service was very nice. The staff were friendly to the passengers. I was seated comfortably and I enjoyed my flight.

When we landed at Egypt International Airport it looked nice and busy. I walked to the transit area where I waited for my connecting flight to Dubai. I met with a lot of South Sudanese traveling to Dubai and I had very nice conversations with them. We shared our stories around. I told one of the passengers that I was talking to about my life experience in South Sudan. When I told him about my prison life story he felt sad about it and he thanked God that I was out of prison.

Soon we all lined up for the next flight to Dubai. I was so excited to go to Australia. After my passport was stamped again at the Egypt International Airport we walked inside the Dubai aeroplane.

The Reflection of my Journey to the Republic of South Sudan

Inside there I realised that I had left my iPad at the Egypt airport transit area. I asked one of the flight attendants and she called security to go and check but they couldn't find it. I was so upset about it. I had a lot of important stuff on it that included my photos of my police training, photos of my journey to my village Bor Town etc.

Luckily, I had been sensible and made a backup of them to my father's computer at his office. That reduced some of the worry.

Soon after takeoff we arrived at Dubai. The journey to Australia from Dubai was about ten hours so I got tired easily.

On the 5th of March 2017 I arrived in Melbourne at seven am. When we landed, I was very happy to see Melbourne again. The weather outside was good as it was nice and warm. I alighted from the plane after several long hours feeling jetlagged. When we walked outside to the waiting area to collect our luggage it was almost an hour long wait. I think they must have been checking the luggage very carefully and perhaps something was wrong.

The airport security staff were standing beside us as we received our bags. I approached the security guard with my phone that I had brought from South Sudan. It was a gift from my friend Jackson Mayiik Chol Guot, my former teacher from the South Sudan National Police College and a very good friend of mine. The security officer told me to turn it on and I did. They took it from me and checked all my photos. They saw my training pictures including me holding an AK47 gun. They started to question me about those pictures and I told them I was doing police training in South Sudan. I was questioned for almost two hours with them. I was increasingly surrounded by more security guards and questioned a lot about my time in South Sudan.

My brother Manyang had been waiting outside for me in the pickup area. My phone was returned back to me and I left with security following me outside. They came with me till I met my

Melbourne, Australia 2017 to now

brother Manyang. We greeted each other warmly feeling happy to see each other again. We got inside the car and drove off. On our way we talked sharing stories.

Finally, I had arrived in Melbourne suburbs again after a long time and we reached the home of my mother and my little sister Thora Malet. They came outside to welcome me.

I was very happy. It was eight am and nice and warm. My father rang on my mum's phone and I spoke to him. He asked if I had arrived safely of course and I told him I did. He was happy to hear that.

A few days later I started to go around to meet with my friends. They all welcomed me back with open arms. Due to my previous work with Victoria police my community members knew me very well. They started to tell me a lot of issues that had been going on with African youths here in Melbourne and clashes with the law and the police. Many of the police members that I had connections with told me about it as well as the police in South Sudan while I was there. I have found that a lot of South Sudanese kids were being locked up in prisons here in Melbourne. This made me feel very sad. There were a lot of African children now in jail. There were also a lot of African children now on the streets, drinking, doing whatever. The majority of them were abusing the freedoms of Australia.

Since I arrived back in Australia on the 5 of March 2017 these sorts of things were very hard for me. I was unemployed and looking for a job around Melbourne for four months. I went around different companies and sent my resume to different workplaces. I was down on my luck but I never gave up. I continued searching for work and was stressing out a lot. I was also receiving a lot of phone calls also from friends and families back home that needed support with money. I didn't have the money to help them out.

Centrelink started to give me 500 AUD every fortnight and I helped those who were in need like Peter Ayuen Lueth Nai.

The Reflection of my Journey to the Republic of South Sudan

He was not the only one who was suffering. There were over 300 South Sudanese soldiers who were suffering with wounds in hospital. Helping all of them was impossible and it made me stressed. Almost half of these wounded people who were in Juba Military Hospital plus some outside hospital had been calling me for help.

This was one of the hardships I had been facing since I have arrived back to Australia. Life became a bit better for me here in Australia compared to my life in South Sudan. My family and friends here in Australia helped me out a lot giving me transport money and weekend money. But it was still hard without a job of course.

My older brother Manyang Malet worked hard to get me the return ticket to come back to Australia. I thought I was not going to make it back to Australia but as you know I did. I have come back now and am feeling happy with my family and friends in Melbourne.

Since I was unsuccessful in getting a job, I began to do some volunteer work with the Salvation Army youth street teams going out on Friday night or Saturday night looking after intoxicated people and the homeless. It was initially just to keep me busy but I came to love it a lot. I see the Salvation Army as one of the best organizations here in Australia. Helping people is what I like.

In September 2017 I decided to do a security course at Braybrook Ashley Street for 17 days. Now I have my security license and I am working in a security department.

Australia is a fascinating country. Not only for me but for many other people as well. Every year countless travellers hit the Australian roads and cities. So, I tried it as well. It was always a dream of mine to go through the country to see the real nature of it. A place where it's often sunny and warm but can be cold and clouds as well. A place where you can go surfing everywhere and any time.

Chapter 27

I returned to Australia from South Sudan on 4th March 2017.

I was still worried that I may be arrested on my arrival because of my court issue.

One day in June 2017 I travelled to Footscray at around two pm. I saw some of police officers patrolling around and as I walked past them, they called me by my brother's name Majok. I replied that I was not Majok but that he was my older brother and they still couldn't believe me. They asked me to produce my ID.

So I served them with my ID document, they checked it and my past court case showed up on their system. Immediately they asked me to go to the Footscray Police Station with them. I agreed and went with them.

After my arrival there they took me to an interview room. I sat down with them and asked them whether it was about the pending court case or something else that I had not completed. They gave me a new court date to go to the Magistrate Court in Melbourne and that was the end of their detention.

I still didn't let anyone in my family or my friends know about the new court date. While waiting for my court date I applied to get my fingerprints for my security license after I finished my Certificate 2 in Security but I was denied a police clearance.

I was so stressed thinking of how to get my security license and commence work but told myself that everything has an end in this world and that one day it would be over.

The Reflection of my Journey to the Republic of South Sudan

I called Sergeant Matt who is a friend of mine and made him aware of what I was facing and asked him to advise me what to do about it. He asked me to organize a catch up with him. I didn't hesitate and told him where to meet me in one of the Ethiopian coffee shops in Footscray.

A day later we met and I showed him all my court papers. From his point of view, he advised me not to stress out too much about it and assured me that it would be ok. He told me to just follow up what the court had told me to do. He told me to take all my support letters along with my anger management certificate and provide them to the Magistrate Court on the day of my attendance.

I started to google where I could possibly do my anger management classes before the court date but most places were very far from where I lived. My struggle was getting bigger and more stressful as I didn't want to go to court without the anger management certificate because it was one of the conditions.

At the last minute I bumped into a friend of mine that I had met in the City of Melbourne sometimes and I asked him where I could do anger management classes in case, he may have an idea. He advised me to go back to court and ask them as they would help me. He was the first person to hear about this court case. I ignored him but continued my googling and I found one in Footscray: The Millennium Medical Centre.

I called them to confirm whether they still offered such qualification. They asked me to come to the office. I immediately left my house for their office.

When I arrived there a polite and kind receptionist welcomed me and asked me what she could help me with. I explained to her why I was there and made sure that she understood it all. She called her boss who was a very nice guy too. They took all my papers and photocopied them and returned the original documents to me. I was subsequently given an appointment to commence counselling services. They told me to come there every Thursday till I completed six sessions of anger management before I received my certificate.

It wasn't hard as I thought. The service was very nice. It had helped me a lot. At the end of the course/sessions I was again asked to pay 360 dollars in order to get my anger management certificate. It was a tough time for me and I didn't have enough money. I had to call some of my friends to help me out. Immediately two of my friends responded positively and three days later I went back to the Millennium Clinic and paid the money and then they emailed me the certificate.

On reception I forwarded it to the Magistrate Court. Afterwards without hesitation I went to the Magistrate Court to confirm whether they had received it or not and all other outstanding documents that I had emailed to them and the answer was yes. I was so happy and please to hear that they had got them.

Finally, my court orders were done and I was a free man again. My stress had gone as there was no criminal records left pending on my name as I was told. I called Sergeant Matt and let him know that my pending court case had finally finished and he then congratulated me. I respect Matt a lot and I see him to be a man of the people, a very respectful man and a man who doesn't have any racial biases. I made him aware of the outcome because he helped me through until the end. He was very happy to hear this great news.

He told me to apply for my fingerprints and the security license. Two weeks later I called to book in for my fingerprint again. I was starting from the beginning again and I was given a new date. Sergeant Matt wasn't only my mentor but also my referee with Doctor Tim from the Footscray Pharmacy.

Dr Tim was introduced to me by Adut Akechak, a South Sudanese young girl who helped me when I was in South Sudan.

The Reflection of my Journey to the Republic of South Sudan

My fingerprints took about three weeks before I received my police clearance which is often required with most job applications. It was clean this time.

Then I applied for my security licence which I was eager to get. It was a long process and now I have it and I am working now as a security guard. I became a free man in the end and I don't have any records under my name.

I learnt a lot from the mistakes I made and I feel wiser now that I will never repeat them. I don't wish to be in trouble with police or to face a Court Judge again.

Chapter 28

On February 17, 2018 I began work as a security guard at the Clique Lounge Bar on 26 King Street in Melbourne. It is open seven days a week from one am on weekdays and from one thirty am on the weekends, closing at eight am or later.

Before I started to work there, I was employed at different venues, mostly on Chapel Street but I like Clique the best.

On my first day, I walked up to the second level and met the manager and club staff and introduced myself as the new security guard. They welcomed me and showed me around and introduced me to the other security guard.

My life has changed a lot since that day. I no longer had the time to meet with my friends on weekends at the nightclubs. I had been partying for ten years and had been to most of the clubs in and outside of Melbourne. There nothing good I can say about that phase of my life. It did turn out to be a learning experience, however.

Sharing what I have learned with future generations is what made me start writing my book. It's a great feeling to share this with people who are ready to learn.

I will repeat this because it is important. My life in Melbourne's nightclub scene wasn't good at all. It was a waste of my time. Today, I am focusing on what is essential in my life.

This is my dream. I want to be a leader. That is why going to work every day makes me feel delighted. I want to work to support myself, my family and even the vulnerable people in South Sudan and elsewhere. I want to stay away from my so-called friends that are doing nothing. I want to stay away from the problems on the street. So, I chose to work through the night. I found it hard at first but now I am used to it and feel very happy about it.

Working as a security guard is stressful sometimes. It's not because of the hours, but because of the people. Some arrive from other venues intoxicated and give us a hard time. In my job, I am obliged to deal with them in a very respectful and responsible way. I must be very careful with them because they are drunk. It's not them talking. It is the alcohol and/or the stress they are under.

Detective Sergeant Matt Illingworth is a good friend of mine who had signed me up to work in his unit at the Sunshine Police station in 2013. I rang him so I could tell him that I was starting work as a security guard. He was very pleased to hear the news.

He then passed on a few words of advice:

"Manyang, congratulations on your security job. Please be careful as you will face a lot of things. Please always use your words and not your hands. Don't ever put your hands on someone."

This same advice was repeated by my older brother Manyang Manyang and many others. I always listen when people take the time to advise me.

Now, I consider their words before acting when there is a problem. Everyone has stress and there is nothing easy in this world. I don't have pressure from work colleagues, the managers or the owner of the club. My stress comes from intoxicated people and people who misbehave in the nightclub. We work as a very good team and always back each other up.

Making money in this world is not easy at all. I must work hard to pay my rent, my bills and to support both my family back home and the people that I help in South Sudan. I must work hard to keep myself busy and to keep me away from my former friends. Work helps me to focus on what's important in my life.

Melbourne, Australia 2017 to now

This why I go to work every time I get rostered on to do so. I am happy that my life has changed. Holding my security licence and working hard makes me very grateful.

Officially, I am employed as a crowd controller with Eagle Security. The owner is very respectful man and a very honest person. I have been employed there for nearly a year now and I am pleased with them.

They understand that sometimes I want to take a day off from work. Before working with them I was employed by another company. I didn't like it though as it was an on-call job. I could go a week without work and was stressing out a lot. With Eagle, I get more hours and my stress is gone.

I spend most of my off hours volunteering with The Salvation Army at 69 Bourke Street in Melbourne and with the Victoria police at the Sunshine Police Station as a liaison officer. I assist in bridging the gap between Victoria police members around the Brimbank area and those in Melbourne City.

With the Salvation Army, I collect money for the Red Shield Appeal and sometimes in their coffee shop where I provide coffee to homeless people. On occasion, I go out on the road and speak with them and try to help. I feel delighted working on gaining something from volunteering time. It's a great experience in my life and I am very proud.

Sometimes I go to work at Clique feeling nervous. I never show it and always make myself busy cleaning up the bar, picking up empty bottles and checking toilets to see if everyone is ok. I also must make sure everyone leaves the venue when it closes. I work safely and I don't want patrons to leave feeling sad or unhappy. I also make sure all the staff are feeling well and go home safely.

I learned this from my father. He treated everyone who came across him very well. How you treat others is generally how they will treat you. The owner of the venue and his staff treat me very well and I treat them well. In my time there, I never heard a bad word from them. They all show me respect.

I worked on my book day and night, every chance I got. Even after I finish work, I am always busy writing my stories on my phone. I write on buses, trains, and especially trams when travelling for long distances. My friends ask me why I always am busy with my phone. I never tell them what I am doing but simply put it away for a bit and talk to them. Later, I return to my writing.

When I write, I like to go where there is a lot of noise such as loud music. I write well in such places. Sometimes I wake up in the middle of the night if I am off work that day and write my stories. I want my stories to be from my heart and I want to share them with people.

Many people want to hear my stories. I had a presentation at the Melbourne Lions Club in late 2018. Most of them found it very sad. I saw one of them crying while I was onstage.

The audience had many questions. Mostly, they asked about a picture on a PowerPoint presentation that showed Ladoli Wani, a disabled child I used to look after when I was in South Sudan. In Australia I still support him by sending him money. His pictures touched those people and made some cry.

After my first stories were edited by my two editors, I went to work feeling delighted after I read them. I was feeling so good that I jumped up and down. The people that saw me in Melbourne City must have been surprised.

One good hearted person came up to me and said: "Brother you look very happy."

I told him very proudly: "Yes I am!"

He wanted to know why, and I was delighted to share it with him. I told him I was writing a book about my journey to South Sudan and that my editors had finally finished with it. He was very happy for me and wanted to hear more. I was pleased to talk about it with him. At the end he pulled out two hundred Australian dollars and gave them to me. In return, I gave him a big hug and said thanks. He went on his way and I headed to work feeling quite happy.

When I reached my workplace, before I signed on and set up the cordon outside, I saw a staff member, a young man named Ben. He is a nice person and a very respectful young man with a good heart. He is also very funny.

He said: "Manyang, you look pleased."

I told him that I was writing a book about my journey to South Sudan. Ben was very happy and willing to hear more. I told him all about it and showed him the pictures of Ladoli Wani and street children that I used to look after when I was in South Sudan. Ben felt quite sad about it.

The staff members some days later asked me about my book. I was happy to recount my journey. Then, the venue manager also called me in to ask the same thing and I told her proudly about my writing. They were pleased for me yet felt sad as well.

Sometimes I go to work feeling very tired because of the amount of time I spend writing. Even now, while composing this, it's 12:40 am I and am still awake.

I really want the world to know about my journey to South Sudan. I want them to know about my struggles and about the people who help me to write my book. My body feels tired but still I am pushing it because I want to show the world my life experiences. I feel very proud.

One day my book will be published by Africa World Books in God's name. I hope that people who will buy it, will read it and learn from it.

When you do good things, one day something good will happen to you. I do my work at the bar with all my heart to make sure everyone in that venue is feeling well and are safe.

The Reflection of my Journey to the Republic of South Sudan

I was approached by the club owners, the manager and the staff. They said that my work is very good they are very pleased to have me there. Hearing such words makes me feel very happy and encourages me to do great things.

All the Clique Bar staff had a meeting when I wasn't there. I had a feeling something was up when I was approached by them in a respectful way. The manager Jodi and the staff told me that they had a discussion amongst themselves about my book and how they could help me to publish it. They said they were happy to put some of their tip money towards book editing and publishing. I nearly cried; I was so happy.

Even the owner of the venue Tom had pledged his support. I had never met him before as he lives in in Queensland. One day he came in while I was working. He approached me with a smile on his face and said he was the owner. I was pleased to meet him. He is a nice person and a very respectful man. Tom asked me about my book as he had heard about it. I told him it was going well, and I was about to finish it.

Jaydee, who works there, one day sat down with me and asked me about my book. I told her a lot and she began to cry. Seeing her being so emotional made me want to stop telling her more as she's a person with a kind heart.

I respect all the people that work at Clique. They are great people with good hearts and are full of humanity and respect.

On Feb. 22, 2019 around four am I was standing at the door on duty. Two South Sudanese boys walked up and I refused them entry because they looked intoxicated. By law I cannot permit them go inside in that state. They also appeared to be very aggressive.

They started to argue with me but I ignored them. They continued to annoy me. My temper became short and I didn't think of what Detective Sergeant Illingworth told me about talking through a situation instead of resorting to violence. I opened the

Melbourne, Australia 2017 to now

velvet rope and started to push one of them away. By law I am not allowed to do that.

One of them got mad at me and then they started to throw punches at me. It was getting out of control. Some of the security guards from the next venue The Centrefold Lounge (a strip club) came to back me up. We managed to get them to the ground. The police were called by one of the other security guards.

King Street has CCTV cameras and the police are always there patrolling to make sure the city is safe. During the fight with the boys I hurt my knees and my right shoulder. There were scrapes and bruises on my knees as I slid down on the ground fighting with them.

Less than five minutes later, two policewomen arrived and arrested one of the boys. The other ran away and turned right on the corner of Flinders Lane and King Street.

The one arrested was arguing with police and completely out of control.

One of the policewomen took my security licence details and asked me for more information. I was not happy about the situation. I took a big breath (my body was shaking afterward) and I gave her a statement that took almost half an hour.

She then went to the station to review the camera footage and see how this issue started. While she did this, I was standing outside talking to the other policewoman. She came back and both policewomen spoke together. As they talked, they reviewed the video that she had downloaded on her phone. They worked out how this case might be closed.

They pulled me aside and told me that I have rights and the two boys also have rights. They were within their rights to punch me as I had put my hands on them first. I was not allowed to do that by law. I had also opened the velvet rope and stepped outside it, which was not allowed at all.

They said I had the right to take this case further if I wanted to, or I could end it there.

I couldn't explain or even ask them more questions. I told them I would end it there. They told me to tell them how I was feeling as I looked sad. I told them I was ok, and we could just close this case. I didn't want to take it further. I repeated it a second time to them.

Before leaving they convinced the boy under arrest to do the same so he could leave the area. After he did so, they come back and tell me goodbye.

A manager, Lana, was on duty on that night. She asked if I was ok. I said yes, I was and told her not to worry. However, inside my heart, I was not ok at all. My heart was burning and I was very sad.

Half an hour later I asked her if I might go home and she said yes. When I went to the office to sign out, I was not feeling well and my head was unfocused. I was still feeling sad about the situation. Instead of taking a tram to St Kilda, I mistakenly took a tram going to Brunswick. Ten minutes later I managed to get off and take the right one.

On the way I received many phone calls from friends who were in the nightclub at the time. They were checking to see that I was ok. When I reached my house my body was still not ok. I had a warm shower, took some painkillers for the bruises and felt a bit better.

Sometimes working as a security guard is not easy at all. It was my first major experience with conflict.

However, in order to put the problem behind me, I asked our security company manager if I could go and work in a different venue for two weeks. I needed to be away from the Clique Bar. He sent me to a place called Toff in Town on Swanston Street in Melbourne. I worked there for a week and I then went to the Billboard night club at 170 Russell St.

After two weeks away from Clique, I missed everyone. The

Melbourne, Australia 2017 to now

Clique Bar is the best place for me, and I love it a lot more than anywhere else. They welcomed me back with great happiness. I was elated to continue my work as normal. I like standing at the door and checking IDs and making sure that everyone who enters are well respected customers.

While on the door the two South Sudanese kids came back. I refused them entry and I told them to come back another time. I said I would let them inside the next time if they behaved well. Before they left, they apologized to me and I accepted their apology.

Three weeks later, they came back and I let them enter. They learned from their mistake and they won't to do that to any security guard again.

Ben spread my story to everyone. He created a tip jug with a small note on it saying it was for donations towards publishing my book. Everyone in the venue could read it and many put money on it. Some patrons have approached me while I was working and asked me about my book. I was proud to talk about it with them. Many people can't wait for it to be published. I never get tired of them asking and always feel happy to discuss it with them.

The manager told me the tip money and donations reached over $1000 AUD. I was thrilled to hear that. It means a lot to me. I really appreciate their support. I work alongside lovely people like Ben, Tom, the owner, Jodi and Lana, the venue managers, and staff members Jaydee, Temp, Shorty, Glen, Harriet and many others.

Together they helped me publish this book: Reflections of My Journey to South Sudan.

Leadership is the ability to facilitate movement in the needed direction and have people feel good about it. Their support means so much to me, and I would like to say thanks to all of them. God bless you all for your help.

Chapter 29

Today I am happy as I am working in security as a security guard and my life has changed completely for the better. It is not like the struggle I had while I was in South Sudan for two years. I would like to extend my big thanks to God and to those who helped me to get my security license.

When I returned to Australia from South Sudan, I kept posting pictures of our three brothers whom I helped while in Juba. Those pictures touched a number of people and then they began to donate some money and other items like wheelchairs.

One of those who helped me a lot is Adut Akechak, a South Sudanese pharmacist in Melbourne.

I keep posting about all three men on my Facebook so that I can keep helping them and letting people know what they need. One day I posted Ladoli Wani's picture on Facebook and one of the South Sudanese men who is a friend of mine on Facebook commented on the picture saying that he was sick and tired of seeing Ladoli Wani pictures every time he was on Facebook.

Some of the other friends on Facebook were offended by his comment and started to argue with him. I remained silent and kept reading their comments. After all the heated debates over, I thanked those who defended my position and stood on my side.

On 28th August 2018 God finally heard my prayers. I woke up early in the morning and I opened my Facebook and I saw a lovely message from this beautiful hearted woman named Julie Hill who lives in America.

Melbourne, Australia 2017 to now

She asked me, "Manyang how can wheelchairs be purchased for the three disabled young men in Juba? Are wheelchairs available for purchase there? I have South Sudanese friends in the US and saw the photos on your Facebook page. My email in the US is julhill@cox.net and thank you for any information."

It was like a dream. I asked myself, is this true? Is Julie really willing to help? I was so excited and energized and extremely happy to hear from people like Julie who wanted to come forward and help these young men, and that was the very reason I kept posting their photos. Before I replied to her, I went to the bathroom with great feelings. I said God has finally heard my prayers.

When I came back from the shower I replied to her message. She replied back too and we continued our conversation on Facebook. Later on, we began to call each other on Messenger. Julie Hill started to ask me more on how we could possibly send those three wheelchairs to Juba, South Sudan.

I told her about my dad being an official at Juba International Airport in South Sudan, specifically a manager in transport and logistics. She was happy to hear that. Inside me I was so happy that the wheelchairs will go to Juba too.

I started to share this great news with my friends and relatives that a woman named Julie Hill from America told me on Facebook that she will provide three wheelchairs for three disabled people I worked with when I was in South Sudan. They all joined in the happiness and felt included in process.

Julie had a friend in Nairobi, Kenya and she was checking on prices there because she found out the other places she checked are only online and had no phone number to call. She said to send her my email address so she can send me pictures of the wheelchairs she got. She said she didn't know how to copy and paste them to Messenger. I sent her my email address and she sent me pictures of the wheelchairs.

The Reflection of my Journey to the Republic of South Sudan

I was very happy to see them and I started to download them and share them on my Facebook page so that all my friends on Facebook could see them too. They were very happy including my elder brother Manyang Malet Manyang. He started to share it with others too.

A few days later Julie Hill sent me a message on Facebook saying "Hi Manyang, I have been away for two days. I must send you the information today about the phone numbers and websites". She said she had talked to my father a few days ago after I sent her his phone number and that my father had said he was going to check on the rates for air shipping from Nairobi to Juba on Kenyan Airways. It became a multi-coordinated project across Australia, America, Kenya and South Sudan. She asked me if I had spoken to my father again. She said she had not called him back yet since they spoke. I replied back confirming my communication with dad after they spoke and that he did check the price he had mentioned in previous communications. We began to make sense and accomplishing something together.

A few days later Julie sent me an email saying:

"Hi Manyang, I received an email from MedEx with partial information on two models of wheelchairs and I replied to them asking for the rest of the information. I have copied it to you so you can see the wheelchairs and my other questions about them. Soon we will have all of the information needed for their purchase and can give your father the weight and dimensions of the cartons for the shipping quote on Kenyan Air. Please let me know when you have received my message and if you are in contact with the three recipients and do you know if they would all want the standard chair. There is a standard and there is a recliner and each are about the same price. The recliner is a padded nylon and it may soak up water in rain so that was not good. The standard chair may be better if they are going to be outside in the rain."

Melbourne, Australia 2017 to now

She also said she would continue chatting with the people in Nairobi to make sure all wheelchairs would reach Juba safely. I thought all was going well between myself and Julie Hill. Happiness had come and I hoped that the wheelchairs would make it to Juba. She was worried if the wheelchairs would reach Juba, South Sudan. I told her they would reach there and my father works at the airport so he would pick them up. That made her feel so please. She started to feel confident that they would reach there safely. I sent her my father's contact number again and she talked to him again and my father explained everything to her.

The wheelchairs were sent to Juba by bus from Nairobi and not by plane because it was cheaper. On the 4th of November 2018 the wheelchairs arrived in Juba and my father received them. When he received them, he called me and he told me that he got wheelchairs, three of them. I was so excited and extremely happy to hear that he had taken possession of the wheelchairs. After I ended the call with Dad, I sent a message straight to Julie Hill to let her know that my father had received the wheelchairs and she joined me in excitement and happiness too. She was always quick to reply back to me. Julie Hill's help meant a lot to me and to those three men who were in need of wheelchairs.

Now Ladoli Wani, Chol Jambo, and Peter Ayuen Lueth have their wheelchairs and they are very happy. Ladoli Wani who used to crawl is no longer crawling and he is making great use of his wheelchair. After accomplishing this mission, Julie wrote an article about why she wanted to help an excerpt of which is included below:

Wheelchairs for three young men

In the summer of 2018, I saw photos on Facebook of three young men in South Sudan who were disabled and without wheelchairs.

Two were in clinic beds, one was sitting in the dirt on the ground, all were in despair. The photos stayed in my mind because in April of 2018 I had lost my own ability to walk and became completely disabled.

After two months in bed, not knowing if I would be confined for the rest of my life, I was approved for an uncommon sacroiliac fusion surgery. Four months post-surgery, I was able to walk and drive again...it was my miracle! While standing at a gas pump for the first time in many months, filling my tank, I stared for a long moment into the sky and realized how much I had missed it. After experiencing my own miracle, I felt compelled to find these young men and help them regain their mobility.

I contacted the stranger on Facebook, Manyang Malet Manyang and learned the identity of the three young men in Juba.

I searched online for a medical supply company in Kenya and purchased three wheelchairs...only $150 a piece! I talked the supply company into allowing one of our Nairobi college students to accompany them on their delivery truck to the bus station to check the chairs onto the bus bound for South Sudan. They were delivered to Juba two days later and picked up by the father of the young man, Manyang, who had posted the Facebook photos. <u>Today all three young men have their wheelchairs!</u>

Ladoli Wani no longer has to drag himself on the ground to get outside. Chol Jambo and Peter Ayuen Lueth are no longer confined to their beds...they are now mobile and can all go outside to see their sky...and their friends.

As Manyang and I spoke many times on Facebook messenger to update each other on our joint project, we discovered that a close cousin of his, a South Sudanese "Lost Girl" who settled in the US, lives just ten minutes from me and is one of my good friends!

All of this was made possible because Manyang listened to his heart and posted the photos of the three young men for me to see

Melbourne, Australia 2017 to now

a world away. He followed his "de-sire" which, translated from Latin, literally means "Of the Father." When your heart whispers for you to help, listen, do not wait, do not seek a second opinion or approval...just do.

How Outreach Africa began

My love for the Sudanese Lost Boys began years before my "chance" meeting with two of them in my local grocery store in Ghent. I took classes in African Cultural Anthropology in College which ignited my passion for African Cultures. I came across photos of Dinka tribesmen of southern Sudan whose eyes showed wisdom and intensity I had never before seen. In the mid-90's I began reading about the Dinka Tribe and their slaughter by the northern Sudanese government which cost over 2.5 million lives, a loss greater than all of our wars combined. I wanted desperately to help them and began sending letters to the International Rescue Committee (IRC) and United Nations High Commission on Refugees (UNHCR) with donations and pleas on their behalf.

Then, in late '98 my life was forever changed by a serious work injury which left me sidelined. For most of the next 3 years I was in constant pain and did not care to live. I was even planning my exit... but then a miracle happened.

Unbeknownst to me, 3,800 Sudanese Lost Boys, whose majority are Dinka, began arriving in the US as war refugees brought over by our government. Just 4 months after their arrival in the US, I discovered Chol and Yaak working in my local grocery store.

It seemed more than chance that I had been brought together with the very people I most wanted to help. God had answered my prayers to help the Dinka and I had found a reason to live. Our non-profit, Outreach Africa: Lost Boys Foundation, was borne of that meeting and has evolved to answer the needs of the Lost Boys and Girls (which includes several other South Sudanese ethnic groups in addition to Dinka). Early on I sponsored 2 of their relatives to boarding school. People in my community joined in and this has evolved into our African Boarding School Program which currently has over 85 of their relatives enrolled in school in Africa. We have already graduated over 130 students and one is now a practicing surgeon in Kenya.

Over the past 17 years of helping the South Sudanese, our small group of 3 volunteers in the US has been able to help so many refugees and displaced people, both here and in Africa. We have raised money for their education, funded life-saving surgeries and rescued entire families by funding their evacuation from burning villages. We network with all of the contacts we have developed in Africa over the years to solve the challenges put before us. We have accomplished these goals, never having set foot in Africa...it is all possible through desire and determination.

I was given a second chance at life when I met the Lost Boys and Girls. When my life seemed unliveable, they gave me purpose and perspective. We have saved each other. The Lost Boys and Girls are my axis; whenever they need me, I will be there. They are my blessing.

Chapter 30

It was back in March 2017 that I just packed my bags, sorted out some personal things, got a ticket for South Sudan and just headed off, with no clue what was waiting for me. Obviously, I tried to inform myself upfront, but as you might know yourself from travelling, you only really get to know a country when you have been there yourself.

Never listen to prejudices. That's one big lesson Australia taught me. And this is what this book is all about. It's about how Australia changed my life and what I have learned through my experience of working with Victoria Police, Melbourne Salvation Army and the Security department. Basically, Australia is a great country for me, personally. And this is why I love this country so much.

It is not just the natural beauty, the exceptional kindness of the Australians and way of living in Down Under, but it is also what living in a country like Australia can teach you about life.

I am proud to be an Australian Citizen. I take Australia as my homeland and a beautiful country. I love how Police work and others that keep Australia to be a nice country. I am very happy to be Australian and live in this country.

Since returning from South Sudan to Melbourne in March 2017. I reunited with many great Australian people including Major Brendan Nottle, Anthony McEvoy (the Manager of Homeless Services at The Salvation Army Project 614) and Lauren Cockerell (the former coordinator of Melbourne Salvation Army Youth Street team's manager). They are the nicest people I have ever met in my entire life.

The Reflection of my Journey to the Republic of South Sudan

The Salvation Army 614 offered me a nice house that I now reside in. Here and around its area is where I am writing this book. It's in the Elwood area and near the beach. It's a very nice area with great people living around me. They are always smiling and welcoming. Australians are very respectful people and friendly to everyone.

In Elwood, Brendan Nottle and Anthony McEvoy made me feel happy and made me love Australia more. I am very happy to have met them in my life's journey here in Australia. I love how people live here in Australia. The Australian people just come up to you and say hello. When you are lost or looking for some places that you have never visited before people often come to you and ask can I help you. Or if you ask them for help, they help you to no end. This has happened to me several times.

I am very proud to be Australian citizen. It just fascinates me how people can be so nice. I think about this a lot. Back home in South Sudan or in Kakuma Refugee Camp where I grew up it's the complete opposite most of the time. Australia changed my understanding. My behaviour changed with as well it in just a short period of time. It just happened too so naturally. When you live in an environment full of friendly and happy people, you become friendly and happy yourself, very quickly.

And this personal change led to other great opportunities. I gained a security job, where I learned countless lessons about myself and other people. I also gained a room in a nice place in Elwood. It's such a nice place where I got to know the coolest people from all over the world. Some guys even came from places I had never heard of before! These guys have such a lovely soul and they still are friends to me today and forever. These people I met around Elwood are those people where you could really see how being a genuine, honest and friendly person leads to having a fulfilled life. You really see it in their eyes and from the way they just live their life.

I really learned a lot on how having the right attitude matters in life. Everything we do with the Salvation Army Youths Street Team is connected to our thoughts and to the way we see things. If you think you can climb a mountain, then you can. If you think you cannot, then you can't. It always just depends on your attitude.

The Salvation Army is the best organization I see to do volunteering work with. I never feel like I am wasting time doing volunteering work with them. I always feel like I am gaining more experience by helping people who are in need of help. It's my happiness to help people like I was helped by UNHCR living as a refugee in Kakuma Refugee Camp for 13 years. This is why I love doing volunteering work with Salvation Army to thank the Australian government back for letting us come to Australia. I would just love to thank God and all the Australian people for their love and for their charity work today. We are living here because Australia is a great country and we South Sudanese are surviving here as a people who have lost their country. I think we have war in South Sudan because we don't have a good enough education system that our people can access.

If only the people of South Sudan could just find a way to live without war. No one will find a way quickly and only dead people have seen the end of the war and the

Today I try to combine the lessons learnt in years we have been living here in Australia with my family. I am very grateful for the lessons I have learned from the people I have met here in Australia. But all this was only possible, because I got out of my comfort zone. I opened up to almost every person that I met. This is the critical requirement that enabled myself to change. If I was not willing to open up and do the things that made me uncomfortable, then I would not have started traveling and learning my journey in life. I see travelling as mostly about opening up, meeting new people, gaining new experiences and eventually becoming a better person. I believe my book can change people who discriminate. They will see and understand better about where they came from and will treat everyone well as it is to be an Australian.

One last small anecdote is that I found that a lot of people who travel to other countries present travelling as this magical holy thing where you start to become a happy person automatically. It seems like many people want to tell you that you truly find yourself while travelling. Travelling to other countries shows and teaches you the way others live and makes adapting their culture and living to be a life changing experience.

Now I have travelled back to South Sudan and returned to Australia I have two difference life experiences of two difference cultures. Travelling I have found is a great teacher. It enables you to find yourself in a way, but it doesn't just happen without pain. You really have to be willing to do it and live it and dwell in it and dig right down into the roots of life. My travels to South Sudan were full of experience. Being sick in South Sudan, being arrested because of helping street children in South Sudan and sentenced to prison because of it, and my life in the Police college in South Sudan and my traveling to my village Bor Town was my experience in my motherland.

Travelling is always fun but can become a little over demanding at times especially as it was for me. It can be really hard at times but just like anything else in life. You can and probably will feel lonely and lost at times. But in these situations, you just need to keep pushing and keep moving. Just don't stop your travels and then you will eventually see, how it changes your life and your perspective on life. When you travel to a foreign country you should respect their culture and their laws that may and most probably will be different to your homeland.

This why I am here in Australia and respecting Australian laws and people who live here in Australia. I am a South Sudanese young man who is now grown up and living here in Australia and loving the country a lot. Eleven years have passed since I came to Australia. In those eleven years, there have been many differences and things that I am not used to. But now I'm having a good time here in Australia.

I feel like I have become more friendly than when I was in South Sudan. In South Sudan, I depended a lot on my parents and good friends, but here I think that I am acting responsibly. My behavior and growing up as an adult and helping poor people back home taught me to be a more responsible person. Unlike South Sudan, I live in a very wide natural environment, so I can relax, and I have become more active and I'm challenging myself more with many things.

I have travelled a lot and it's of great interest to me. I like to learn and assist in the area of security. I am trained in the same and I have a lot of experience now. I like the challenges of working in a sometimes-stressful environment. I enjoy working with different cultures and the public. I love the fact that there's a job that gives you the chance to help out and keep people safe wherever you go and whatever you do. To protect the public, the buildings, the infrastructure is of great interest for me. I love security work a lot and I am enjoying it.

My life in Australia is great, a very good life and I have met numerous people who are very concerned much about my life. I met people like Sergeant Reece Campbell who I did roadwork with and working with Reece was a really great experience. We did a lot of police work around the Sunshine areas keeping Sunshine safe.

I also met Sergeant Matt Illingworth. Sergeant Matt was a uniform Sergeant at Sunshine back then but now he is a Detective Sergeant in Victoria Police Crime Command and I feel very proud in seeing him moving up and I hope one day to see him in Chief Commissioner uniform. I also met Inspector Tony Long

The Reflection of my Journey to the Republic of South Sudan

Superintendent Police Michael Grainger, Inspector Christ Gilbert. Aaron Heriot and Glenn McFarland.

The last two invited me to do a presentation during a Melbourne East Police members training day. The presentation was about the war in South Sudan and about our life in different refugee camps and a bit about our new life here in Australia. Many members felt sad understanding how hard was the life journey from our homeland to Australia. I became well known by many of our police in Melbourne through my presentations with Victoria Police members and they have learned a lot from me.

I also met with Assistant Police Commissioner Andrew Crisp and Lieh Trinh the Manager of Victoria Police Crime Stoppers. Lieh and I been doing a lot of presentations around Sunshine, Footscray and Dandenong areas giving awareness talks about crime and about Crime Stoppers to primary schools and secondary schools in 2013 and mid 2014. It was great working with different units of Victoria Police.

I also met Inspector Trevor King Acting Sergeant Johnny Collard, Ash Dixit, Moses Lado and Richard Dove.

Richard Dove had written a book about Burmese people coming to Australia that he gave me a copy of in 2013. I enjoyed reading it a lot. I don't believe that if you do good, good things will happen. I believe everything is completely accidental and random. Sometimes bad things happen to very good people and sometimes good things happen to bad people. But at least if you try to do good things, then you're spending your time doing something worthwhile.

Living in Australia and meeting all these great people I have mentioned here has made me feel very happy. They all took their time to teach me how to begin a new life here in Australia. The purpose of writing this book is to let other people who live here in Australia or other countries know the hardship people are struggling with in South Sudan. I want to let other South Sudanese who cross the oceans coming to Australia or even born in here know that they are in a better country here in Australia. This country is the best country. I suffered a lot when I was in South Sudan seeing people dying of malaria, starvation and seeing street children and people with disabilities suffering in South Sudan. Being sent to prison because of helping street children and people with disabilities.

But never lose hope. I believe one day the government of South Sudan will understand the great work I was doing to help vulnerable people in my motherland. I still believe and have hope I will help my country one day. I believe I will be a leader for the poor in South Sudan one day. Australia is the dream of many travelers and therefore I know that there will be a lot of people not sharing my opinion, but I can hope that perhaps they may change.

One day we are all going to enjoy the benefits of our motherland South Sudan and welcome others like Australian people to our motherland. I hope we can give them a citizenship to be citizens in my homeland just as I am Australian citizen living here happily in Australia. Australia is my third country. I love it a lot. I don't know what to say more about it but I can only say that I love Australia.

Now I am here in this book sharing this with our South Sudanese kids who live here in Australia. Many of them may never travel back to South Sudan so this book provides some opportunity to let them learn through my life experience. My book is named "The reflections of my Journey to South Sudan" Hopefully through it others can have some knowledge of the country South Sudan.

Publishing this book makes me feel very happy because I am giving other people knowledge of my motherland and my life experiences that I have been through. I feel proud of myself. To my editor, my secondary school teacher, who wishes to remain anonymous, today I feel very proud because of you. I've also

The Reflection of my Journey to the Republic of South Sudan

come to love writing, reading, and writing a book because you gave me the strength, the spirit, the confidence I needed to take the next steps toward my dream of acting and writing. I'm so grateful you were my teacher and you gave me your knowledge through teaching me the opportunities available out there to be a better person. Thank you for encouraging me. Your positivity and encouragement brightened my days. You made me a better, more thoughtful, person. Your kindness made me feel welcomed to Australia and more comfortable. I'll never forget you. You gave me the confidence to dream big. Thank you for your patience throughout these years I have spent in Australia. It meant the world to me. I had a hard time at high school. But you still helped. You are, hands down, the best teacher I've ever had. You didn't give up on me. You inspired me to begin this new chapter in my life. I wouldn't have done it without you. I'll always remember attending your class. You were the best teacher.

My book has also been inspired by one of my childhood brothers Jok Makuach. Jok was the one who pushed me to write this book after I shared my journey with him.

My book will teach and inspire other South Sudanese who have never been back to South Sudan and other Australians who have never heard our stories before. Once again thanks to those who helped, thanks to those in my story and to my book readers. Thanks for reading about my journey and I hope you have learnt something from my experience and enjoyed just simply reading it.

Photographs from my Journey

The Reflection of my Journey to the Republic of South Sudan

My Aunty Arual in her cattle's camp.

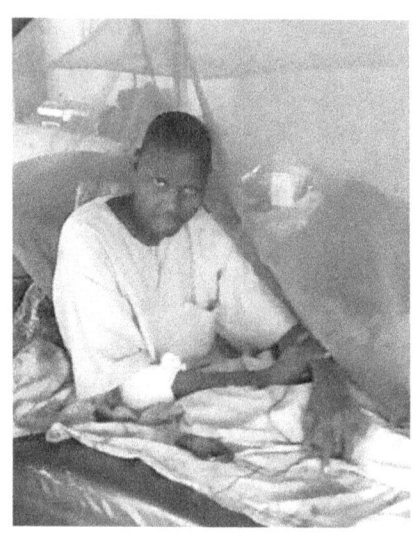

Peter Ayuen Lueth – the first photo when I met him in Juba Military Hospital.

Ladoli Wani crawling back to his house after we had tea together.

After I had a dream about Ladoli Wani, this is the very first picture I took when I met him.

The Reflection of my Journey to the Republic of South Sudan

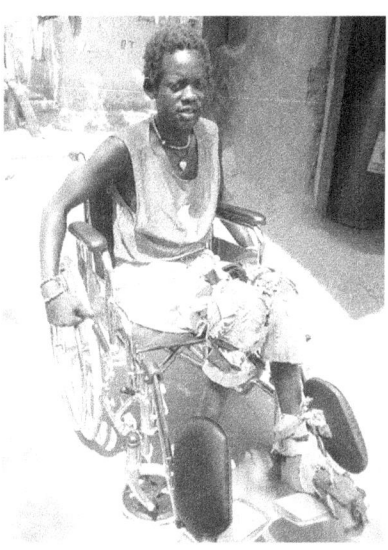

Ladoli Wani today in his new wheelchair.

Ladoli Wani with his mother and his aunties feeling happy at their house in Juba, South Sudan.

The Reflection of my Journey to the Republic of South Sudan

Myself and my former colleagues at Rajaaf National Police College.

Myself and Detective Sergeant Matt at Sunshine Police Sation in 2013.

Me at Rajaaf National Police College.

The Reflection of my Journey to the Republic of South Sudan

Peter Ayuen Lueth with my father, Enock Malet Manyang at Juba Military Hospital.

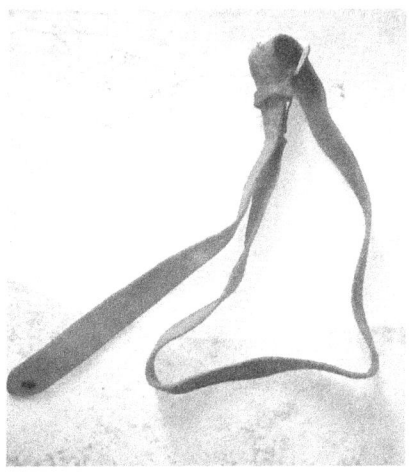

I got this belt from my father as a gift in 2005 when I was coming to Australia with my family. I still have it today.

The Reflection of my Journey to the Republic of South Sudan

At the front gate of Rajaaf National Police College coming out from Rajaaf Hospital – I was sick.

I was among this group on this vehicle for my last journey to Bor Town on November 19th, 2019.

Myself and General Pieng Deng Kuol, the former IGP Inspector General of South Sudan Police. We took this picture during the CID graduation day at Rajaaf National Police College.

The Reflection of my Journey to the Republic of South Sudan

The road to my home town, Bor Town is full of dust and small rocks.

Sharing food with street children in South Sudan was a great happiness in my life.

Me and Salvation Army Major Branden Nottle, a very respectful man who always has a smile.

Volunteering with the Salvation Army 614 for seven years is the greatest happiness of my life.

The Reflection of my Journey to the Republic of South Sudan

My last journey to my home town was sad.

The road to my home town was not safe at all.

The Reflection of my Journey to the Republic of South Sudan

I am being welcomed to my home town Bor Town by this lovely people – I was very happy to meet them.

I look like a skeleton in Rajaaf National Police College.

Our life in Rajaaf National Police College – my former colleagues are among this group.

The Reflection of my Journey to the Republic of South Sudan

I have a dream that one day I want to be a leader of the vulnerable people in South Sudan.

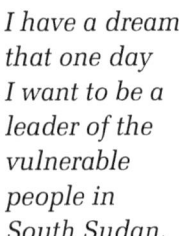

The Reflection of my Journey to the Republic of South Sudan

LEFT: My father, Enock Malet Manyang, my mother, Abuk Chagai and me at Juba International airport when I was returning to Australia.

BELOW LEFT: With my grandfathers in Bor Town.

BELOW RIGHT: With my grandmother, Keithdit. This was the first time in my life to meet her in Bor Town. She passed away in 2016 before I came back to Australia.

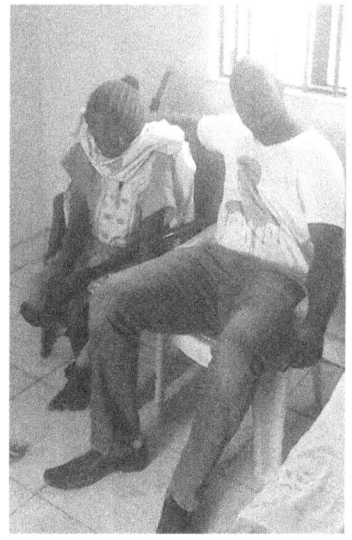

The Reflection of my Journey to the Republic of South Sudan

LEFT: Donating soup to wounded soldiers in Juba Military Hospital.

BELOW LEFT: Abu Sallah the first street child I rescued in South Sudan. He was starving and sick. Read more about him in the book.

BELOW RIGHT: Chol Jambo, one of the wounded soldiers who I used to help in Juba Military Hospital.

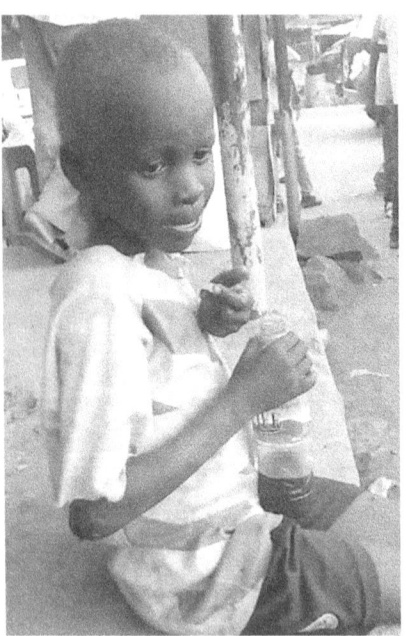
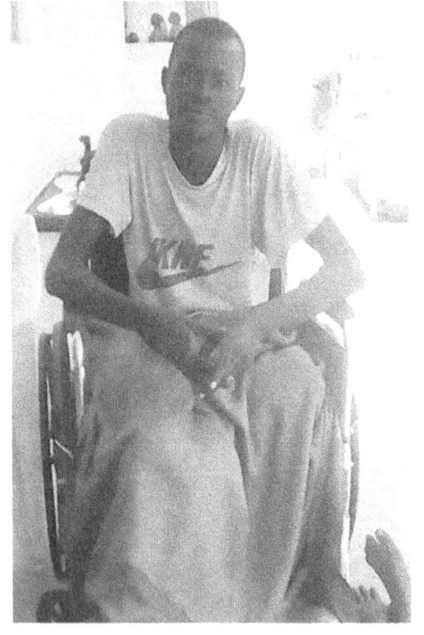

The Reflection of my Journey to the Republic of South Sudan

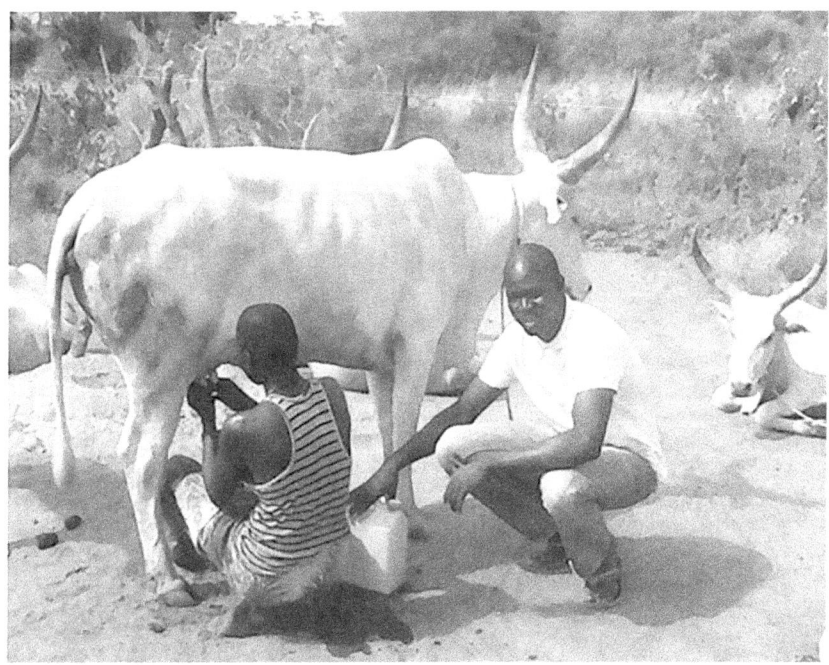

My Aunty Arual milking cow in the traditional way. I am next to her.

My grandmother, Mary Adhieu Mayom Ayiik's grave. I took this picture when I first visited her graveyard.

The Reflection of my Journey to the Republic of South Sudan

My book was being supported by my workplace staff, managers and the owners.

www.ingramcontent.com/pod-product-compliance
Lightning Source LLC
Chambersburg PA
CBHW051945290426
44110CB00015B/2118